F. R. Leavis

Two Cultures?
The Significance of C. P. Snow

with Introduction by
Stefan Collini

~

CAMBRIDGE
UNIVERSITY PRESS

CAMBRIDGE
UNIVERSITY PRESS

University Printing House, Cambridge CB2 8BS, United Kingdom

Published in the United States of America by Cambridge University Press,
New York

Cambridge University Press is part of the University of Cambridge.

It furthers the University's mission by disseminating knowledge in the pursuit
of education, learning and research at the highest international levels of
excellence.

www.cambridge.org
Information on this title: www.cambridge.org/9781107617353

© Cambridge University Press 2013

First published 2013
Reprinted 2019

Printed in the United Kingdom by TJ International Ltd. Padstow Cornwall

A catalogue record for this publication is available from the British Library

Library of Congress Cataloguing in Publication data
Leavis, F. R. (Frank Raymond), 1895–1978.
Two cultures? : the significance of C.P. Snow / F.R. Leavis ; with introduction
by Stefan Collini.
pages   cm
Includes bibliographical references.
ISBN 978-1-107-61735-3 (pbk.)
1. Snow, C. P. (Charles Percy), 1905–1980. Two cultures and the scientific
revolution.   2. Science and the humanities.   I. Collini, Stefan, 1947–
II. Title.
AZ361.S57L4   2013
823'.912 – dc23   2013017282

ISBN 978-1-107-61735-3 Paperback

CONTENTS

Introduction

∼

'There can be no two opinions about the tone in which Dr Leavis deals with Sir Charles. It is a bad tone, an impermissible tone.' Lionel Trilling's magisterial judgement expressed a very widely held view. Both at the time and since, F. R. Leavis's critique of C. P. Snow's 'The Two Cultures and the Scientific Revolution' was and has remained a byword for excess – too personal, too dismissive, too rude, too Leavis. Whatever view they have taken of the limitations and confusions of Snow's original contentions – and Trilling, among others, itemized a good many – commentators on this celebrated or notorious 'exchange' (if it can be called that: there was little real give and even less take) have largely concurred in finding the style and address of Leavis's scathing criticism to be self-defeating. Aldous Huxley denounced it as 'violent and ill-mannered', disfigured by its 'one-track moralistic literarism'. Even reviewers sympathetic to some of Leavis's criticisms recoiled: 'Here is pure hysteria'.[1]

'It will be a classic' was Leavis's own, surprisingly confident, judgement on his lecture.[2] Though few of its

---

[1] Lionel Trilling, 'Science, literature, and culture: a comment on the Leavis–Snow controversy', *Commentary* (June 1962), 462–3; Aldous Huxley, *Literature and Science* (New York: Harper & Row, 1963), p. 1; Hilary Corke, 'The dog that didn't bark', *New Republic* (13 April 1963), 28.

[2] When Cambridge University Press proposed that the lecture would need to be toned down before they could publish it, Leavis refused,

I

early readers concurred – the lecture was more commonly seen as a classic example of intemperate abuse – with the passage of time the merits of its criticisms of Snow and what Snow represented have started to become better appreciated. In particular, the character of Leavis's performance and the genre to which it belongs have come into focus more clearly as the contingent elements of personality and newsworthiness have fallen away. Now, half a century after its initial delivery (as the Richmond lecture at Downing College Cambridge in 1962), it is appropriate to consider whether Leavis's lecture should indeed be seen as a minor classic of cultural criticism – a still pertinent illustration both of the obstacles faced by the critic who understands himself to be challenging a set of attitudes that are so widely shared and so deeply rooted as to seem to most members of that society to be self-evident truths, and of the discursive tactics and rhetorical resources appropriate to this difficult task. It is surely telling that both the pieces reprinted here have question marks in their titles, calling some piece of received wisdom or usage into doubt.

Although much of the immediate response to the Richmond lecture saw it as an unpardonably personal attack, Leavis always insisted that he was concerned with something much larger than the merits or failings of one individual. And although the episode is usually referred to as 'the two cultures controversy', Leavis also insisted that he was not primarily offering a commentary on the

adding: 'I've looked through the lecture again and am bound to say that I've done better than I should have thought possible. I can't help saying, modestly, that it will be a classic.' Letter of 1 May 1962, quoted in Ian MacKillop, *F. R. Leavis: A Life in Criticism* (London: Allen Lane, 1995), p. 323.

disciplinary character and claims of the humanities as opposed to the sciences, still less asserting the educational or institutional priority of one over the other, and most certainly not denying the huge importance of science in the modern world. His real target was neither a particular individual nor a set of educational arrangements. It was, in the first instance, the dynamics of reputation and public debate – the ways in which certain figures are consecrated as bearers of cultural authority. But beyond that, it was, centrally, the axiomatic status accorded to economic prosperity as the exclusive or overriding goal of all social action and policy. Fifty years later, the relevance or urgency of analysing this dynamic and contesting this status can hardly be said to have diminished.

Although the idea of 'the two cultures', or perhaps just the phrase itself, may seem to have entered the bloodstream of modern culture, the circumstances under which it was launched on its global career may now, for most readers, require historical recovery and reconstruction.[3] 'The two cultures and the scientific revolution' was delivered as the Rede lecture at Cambridge University in May 1959. The two cultures of the title were those of the natural scientists and of what the lecture sometimes referred to as 'the literary intellectuals', sometimes as 'the traditional culture'. C. P. Snow[4] was taken to speak with authority

---

[3] I attempted to supply this in more detail in the introduction to the Canto edition of Snow's lecture (*The Two Cultures* (Cambridge University Press, 1993), to which the present edition supplies the companion volume).

[4] Leavis's subtitle referred to 'C. P. Snow', which is how he was widely known, especially as a novelist. But in 1957 Snow had been knighted, and so in the text Leavis frequently refers to him as 'Sir Charles Snow', which is how he is also styled in the title of Michael Yudkin's piece

on both cultures, having begun his career as a research scientist in the Cavendish Laboratory at Cambridge (and subsequently played an important role in recruiting scientists into the Civil Service), but having latterly become best known as a novelist. The core of his argument was that the application of science and technology, and the prosperity that was presumed to follow, offered the best hope for meeting mankind's fundamental needs, but that this goal was being frustrated by the gulf of ignorance between the two cultures and the educational arrangements that, especially in Great Britain, perpetuated this divide. Snow made it clear that he believed the literary intellectuals, representatives of the traditional culture, were largely to blame for this deplorable situation: while the scientists had 'the future in their bones', the literary intellectuals were 'natural Luddites'.

In its published form, the Rede lecture provoked a great deal of discussion, both in Britain and elsewhere, and its success confirmed Snow in his role as a sage or pundit who was licensed to pronounce on the great issues of the day. (Such was his standing in the early 1960s that he was invited by Harold Wilson to become a minister in the newly created Ministry of Technology following the 1964 election, despite never having held any elected office or other political position.) It was these matters of reputation – Snow's standing as a cultural authority as

reprinted with the Richmond lecture in the Chatto edition. Snow accepted a peerage in 1964, and in reprinting his lecture in 1972, Leavis modified its subtitle accordingly, though without changing the form of the references to Snow in the text. Since his death he has nearly always been referred to as 'C. P. Snow', and so Leavis's title is here given in its original form.

much as the content of his claims – that Leavis was to address in the first of the lectures republished here.

Leavis's life and career

Frank Raymond Leavis was born in Cambridge in 1895, of relatively humble social origins, and, aside from service as a medical orderly with a Quaker ambulance unit in the First World War, he was to spend his entire life there. As an undergraduate, he switched from History to the newly established course in English, graduating with first-class honours in 1921. He then undertook a PhD, at the time a novel and unusual route in British academic life: as a result, he was always referred to as 'Dr Leavis', a title which could, in the delicately layered nuances of social interchange in mid twentieth-century Britain, be made to carry connotations of abstruse academicism or even the lack of a desirable kind of effortless *sprezzatura*. He made his way slowly in Cambridge, for several years supporting himself as a freelance college teacher; only in 1936 did he obtain a full fellowship, at Downing College, and only in 1945, when he was already fifty, was he finally confirmed in a fully-salaried university appointment (he was never made a professor). In 1932 he and a group of younger associates founded the journal *Scrutiny*, of which he (supported by his wife and fellow critic Q. D. Leavis) remained the effective editor until its closure in 1953. The journal's rigorous, unyielding critical judgements and stinging cultural critiques drew a devoted following in the middle decades of the century, Leavis taking particular pride in the fact that it had no official status or support. Temperamentally inclined to see himself as an outsider, he even referred, with memorable excess, to those who had collaborated on the journal as 'outlaws'.[5]

Leavis cultivated a particularly strenuous form of criticism in which close attention to the verbal texture of works of literature was underwritten by an intense preoccupation with the human quality of the life expressed in that writing. Such criticism, Leavis insisted, was the core of any worthwhile study of English literature – its place could not be taken by the accumulation of biographical or historical knowledge *about* literature – and such criticism rested, at bottom, on unflinchingly personal judgements of quality. Extending these concerns, he also developed a wide-ranging critique of the form of society that had resulted from the Industrial Revolution and the growth of 'mass civilization'. The experience of humanly satisfying work and membership of settled communities had largely been lost, replaced by machine-governed labour, empty consumerism and anomic individualism. In Leavis's view, one particular casualty of these social changes was the loss of an effective educated public capable of sustaining genuine standards of criticism; he despaired of the superficiality and mutual back-scratching of contemporary literary culture, and thought that the only hope for the future lay in the formation in the university of a minority public capable of true critical discrimination. In all kinds of ways, therefore, Snow and Snow's success brought together several of the themes that most deeply exercised Leavis.

Despite the volume of attention Snow's lecture received, Leavis initially made no public comment about

---

5 F. R. Leavis, 'A retrospect', in *Scrutiny: A Quarterly Review*, 20 vols. (Cambridge University Press, 1963), vol. XX, p. 218.

it. According to his own later report, he had glanced at it – and concluded that he need do no more. But he may have been irked by others associating his favoured form of realism in fiction with that (actually rather different kind) practised by Snow in his own novels, and he was certainly irked by the way in which the Rede lecture started to crop up in essays written for Cambridge entrance scholarships.[6] He finally read it in the summer of 1961, just before his last year of teaching in Cambridge (he was to retire from his university post at the end of the summer of 1962), and early in that academic year he was invited by the undergraduates of his own college, Downing, to deliver the annual Richmond lecture. Leavis decided to take Snow, and the Rede lecture in particular, as his topic, and in January 1962 he reported that he was investing as much thought and energy into his preparations as into anything he had previously written.[7] The lecture was announced for 28 February.

By this point in his career, Leavis's reputation as a fierce and formidable critic extended beyond academia, so the occasion was regarded by the press as newsworthy and the BBC requested permission to broadcast the lecture. Leavis resisted all such approaches: 'There can be no question of recording my lecture, or using it for any BBC purpose.'[8] It was to be a purely internal college occasion. But, inevitably, the packed hall contained

[6] On the former, see Guy Ortolano, *The Two Cultures Controversy: Science, Literature, and Cultural Politics in Postwar Britain* (Cambridge University Press, 2009), pp. 93–4; on the latter, see Leavis's comment below (page 56).

[7] G. Singh, *F. R. Leavis, A Literary Biography* (London: Duckworth, 1995), p. 288.

[8] Leavis to the BBC, 27 February 1962; quoted in MacKillop, *Leavis*, p. 317.

people from other colleges, including the *Times*' 'Cambridge Correspondent' (probably the classicist L. P. Wilkinson of King's) and the historian J. H. Plumb from Christ's, one of Snow's closest friends. A report of the occasion appeared in the *Times* on 1 March and in the *Sunday Times* two days later. It is still not entirely clear what happened next, but the *Spectator*, a weekly periodical of right-leaning if sometimes maverick political and cultural analysis, announced in its issue of Saturday, 2 March that the full text of Leavis's lecture would appear the following week. It would seem that Iain Hamilton, the journal's literary editor, was instrumental in securing permission to publish it. Hamilton took legal advice on whether publication might involve the risk of a suit for libel, so defamatory of Snow's professional reputation were passages in the lecture. Counsel's opinion was that there would indeed be *prima facie* grounds for such a case, and that publication should only go ahead if Snow's written consent were obtained in advance. Snow was sent the lecture; he was, apparently (and quite understandably), 'nettled' by some of it, but did not try to prevent publication.[9]

The full text appeared in the *Spectator* on 9 March, illustrated with some rather unflattering drawings of Snow (and one, less unflattering, of Leavis). It was prefaced by a short note by Leavis which explained: 'The appearance in the newspapers of garbled reports has made it desirable that the lecture should appear in full.' Its publication provoked a storm of comment; for some weeks the

[9] For details, see MacKillop. *Leavis*, pp. 321–2; Ortolano, *Two Cultures Controversy*, pp. 96–9. For Snow's own later version of events, see his *Public Affairs* (New York: Scribner's, 1971), pp. 84–6.

Spectator carried pages of letters most (but not all) of which expressed outrage at both the tone and content of Leavis's attack, and this was only the beginning of the widespread condemnation referred to earlier. In revisiting the episode now, we need not only to ask what it was about Leavis's performance that provoked this storm, but also to consider whether some of those who rushed to judgement of the lecture may have misconstrued its larger purpose.

'Two cultures?'

'If confidence in oneself as a master-mind, qualified by capacity, insight and knowledge to pronounce authoritatively on the frightening problems of our civilization, is genius, then there can be no doubt about Sir Charles Snow's' (53).[10] It is, by any measure, an arresting opening sentence. It immediately announces that Snow's claim to speak with authority is the question at issue. And at the same time it begins the process of undermining that claim by implying that it rests on little more than self-ascribed status born out of a soaring belief in his own capacities. Moreover, it manages to suggest that the belief is misplaced: no competent reader could doubt that the character and validity of Snow's claim are being ironized, though it might be difficult at first to point to the specifics of vocabulary and syntax by which this effect is achieved. The choice of 'genius' as the pivotal word of the sentence is deadly, as is the related use of 'master-mind': the high register of these terms is likely to raise eyebrows, an

---

[10] The page numbers embedded in the text refer to Leavis's lecture as printed in the present edition.

impression reinforced by the circular structure of the sentence. The irresistible implication is that Snow thinks of himself in these grandiose terms, and indeed that it is only because he holds this exalted view of his own talents that he has been accorded such deferential attention.

The rest of the first paragraph powerfully reinforces this implied judgement:. 'Of course, anyone who offers to speak with inwardness and authority on both science and literature will be conscious of more than ordinary powers'. Already the suspicion is raised that the powers, as opposed to the self-belief, may in reality be no more than ordinary. But Snow writes as though he has no doubts on these matters, and it is to the *tone* of Snow's pronouncements that Leavis addresses one of the most withering sentences in a relentlessly withering performance: 'The peculiar quality of Snow's assurance expresses itself in a pervasive tone; a tone of which one can say that, while only genius could justify it, one cannot readily think of genius adopting it.' And there, we cannot help but feel, we have Snow. That 'assurance' is the defining quality of his public persona, but it is devastatingly misplaced. The very fact of his deliberately cultivating the tone of a 'master-mind' decisively indicates that he is not one.

Although at this point we are only four sentences into the Richmond lecture, a tone quite unlike Snow's is already in evidence – sardonic yet also angry, sceptical yet unyielding. Nothing has been said of the content of Snow's claims: his standing as an authority is the focus, and, above all, the tone through which his sense of that standing is expressed. Tone is, of course, the home turf of the literary critic, and Leavis's analysis is laced with acute and apt brief characterizations of Snow's style, 'with its show of giving us the easily controlled spontaneity of the great man's talk' – a telling description which already begins to expose the sham of the 'show'. The first passage quoted from the Rede lecture damns itself irretrievably when held up in Leavis's tweezers:

The only writer of world-class who seems to have had an understanding of the industrial revolution was Ibsen in his old age: and there wasn't much that old man didn't understand.

On which Leavis comments: 'Clearly, there is still less Sir Charles Snow doesn't understand: he pays the tribute with authority' (53). Selecting the telling quotation is one of the hallmark skills (or, in some cases, weapons) of literary criticism. Leavis acknowledges the limitations of illustrating tone by means of a single sentence, but his choice is deadly: the longer one stares at Snow's statement, the more egregious its multiple fatuities become. And Leavis's comment draws attention to the central theme of his critique: well before the end of the first page, the question of 'authority' has been raised three times, with clear intent.

The Richmond lecture has frequently been misperceived as a purely personal attack on Snow or as a simple reversal of the case Snow had (at least implicitly) made for the priority of the scientific culture over the literary. But Leavis's purpose was neither as petty as the first of these, nor as academic as the second. His opening sentences are not introductory to a purpose yet to be revealed: they provide a powerful epitome of it.

The first task, therefore, that Leavis set for himself was to challenge and correct the overestimation of Snow as a sage. It was not a task Leavis showed any inclination to shirk. 'Snow is in fact portentously ignorant'; 'Snow exposes complacently a complete ignorance'; 'he is as intellectually undistinguished as it is possible to be'; and more in similar vein (we are not yet at the end of the second page). In himself, Snow is 'negligible', but, in being taken as a sage, he is a portent: 'His significance is that he has been accepted – or perhaps the point is better made by saying "created": he has been created as authoritative intellect by the cultural conditions manifested in his acceptance' (54). The somewhat dense circularity of this last phrase is characteristic both of Leavis's prose more generally and of his particular case in this lecture. The significance of Snow lies, according to Leavis, precisely in what his unmerited elevation tells us about the society which has accorded him such standing. So, Leavis is not 'replying' to Snow: 'It is not any challenge he thinks of himself as uttering, but the challenge he *is*, that demands our attention.' Leavis is only turning, belatedly and reluctantly, to an examination of the Rede lecture because it quickly 'took on the standing of a classic' (even here he is unwilling to collude with the process by saying it 'became' a classic). The fact that schoolteachers were making their university scholarship candidates read it seems to have been the final straw, given the hopes Leavis invested in recruiting the brightest products of the country's sixth forms.

So, Snow's 'claim to authority' must be challenged. The first leg to be kicked away has to be his standing as a novelist; this, after all, underwrites his unique position as one fitted to speak with equal authority on literature as well as on science. Leavis is unsparing: 'Snow is, of course, a – no, I can't say that; he isn't; Snow thinks of himself as a novelist' (57). Retaining the cadence of the speaking voice in print can be hazardous, but here the arrest in the middle of the sentence enacts the questioning of the received description. Snow has published books classified as novels, but how far, when judged by the standards of the great practitioners of the genre, does he really have the root of the matter in him? Leavis's answer is offensively extreme – and deliberately so, of course: 'as a novelist he doesn't exist; he doesn't begin to exist. He can't be said to know what a novel is'. Any reader already disposed to feel uncomfortable with Leavis's uncompromising assault on Snow's reputation may flinch a little at this point. Even if one does not regard Snow as a great novelist, is it really necessary to be so utterly dismissive? Leavis only compounds his offence, suggesting, in an unconvincing attempt at humour, that he has heard that the novels are 'composed for him by an electronic brain called Charlie' (perhaps faintly echoing the selection of winning Premium Bond numbers by a computer called 'Ernie' that had been introduced a few years earlier). In truth, the failings in Snow's novels that Leavis goes on to itemize would probably now be acknowledged by most critics: he 'tells' rather than 'shows'; much of his dialogue is almost literally unspeakable; his characters are wooden and stereotypical; and so on. Nonetheless, to say of an author who had by this point sold many thousands of copies that 'as novelist he doesn't exist' smacks of shock tactics, as indeed it was intended to do.

Kicking away the other leg from under Snow's standing, that of being a highly qualified scientist, might seem to have been a more difficult task for Leavis, as a literary critic, to accomplish. But he does not hesitate. Having observed, again with some justice, that there is no sign in the novels that Snow 'has really been a scientist, that science as such has ever, in any important inward way, existed for him', he goes on to insist that it is equally absent from the Rede lecture. 'Of qualities that one might set to the credit of a scientific training there are none.' In their place all we get is 'a show of knowledgeableness'. It's a severe, even haughty, phrase, but any reader of Snow's essays and journalism is likely to recognize some truth in it. Snow *asserts* that what he calls the scientific culture 'contains a great deal of argument, usually much more rigorous, and almost always at a higher conceptual level' than the literary culture, but he conspicuously fails, according to Leavis, to *exhibit* these alleged strengths in his own work. One reason why, when he came to publish the Richmond lecture in pamphlet form, Leavis took the unusual step of including Michael Yudkin's essay with it was precisely because it illustrated how practising scientists (Yudkin was a young biochemist) were equally unwilling to allow Snow to wear the mantle of science's champion.[11] His title to that role has been further undermined by the fuller biographical picture of Snow's early career that has emerged since his death, which has underscored that, far from being able to speak on the basis of distinguished and extensive research achievements of his own, his period as a practising scientist had been relatively brief and not uniformly successful; his turn to other careers may not have been quite as freely chosen as he later liked to imply.

[11] See below, A Note on the Text. Yudkin's quizzical – and at times downright critical – essay on Snow's lecture had originally been published in the *Cambridge Review*. Leavis read it only after he had delivered the Richmond lecture – 'I saw it would go with mine beautifully' – and asked Yudkin's permission to reprint it alongside his own text; see MacKillop. *Leavis*, p. 323.

As Leavis proceeds with his indictment, turning next to Snow's loose use of the category of 'culture', he makes an observation in passing whose methodological significance for the whole activity of cultural criticism is substantial. He allows that in the matters under discussion 'thought... doesn't admit of control by strict definition of the key terms', and then goes on: 'but the more fully one realizes this the more aware will one be of the need to cultivate a vigilant responsibility in using them, and an alert consciousness of any changes of force they may incur as the argument passes from context to context' (60). This may seem the merest common sense, a maxim of critical hygiene, but for Leavis, as we shall see, it also signals an important tactical principle. Stipulative definition of abstract terms is of very little value – indeed it may get in the way of deeper thinking – even though one's opponents may demand that one's position be given crisp and definitive formulation. Instead, the cultural critic cultivates and, by example and even by irritating obstructiveness, incites others to cultivate, a restless dissatisfaction with abstract terms, a mindful awareness of the reductive or Procrustean potential of all general formulations. This is, or should be, home territory for the literary critic, and points to a distinctive role in public debate – or at least, to a form of engagement in which a more than ordinary attentiveness to language functions, not as a distracting fastidiousness, but as the active embodiment of positive values and the only way such values can be made effective in controversy. It is as part of this engagement that Leavis describes the Rede lecture as 'a document for the study of cliché' (62).

Cliché results from repetition, and a proposition that is repeated frequently and generally enough acquires the status of the self-evident. Leavis suggests that Snow is a 'portent', and thus merits examination precisely because he is so *un*original. Snow utters his platitudes with such self-confidence in part because they seem, to him and to many of his readers, to be so obviously true. These are what Leavis calls 'currency values', the verbal coin that is rubbed smooth by being constantly circulated in a particular social world. He sees this as almost a closed system: to be recognized by this social world as saying something sensible and significant one needs to endorse its currency values, and the fact of their being so repeatedly endorsed is what confirms them in their status as self-evident truths. Leavis, here and elsewhere in his writings, comes perilously near to the self-dramatizing pessimism of 'the outsider' who suggests that it is *impossible* to obtain a hearing for an alternative perspective, so sealed and self-reinforcing is this system. And yet, by the very fact of his critical writing he is tacitly assuming that there *is* an audience capable of recognizing the truth of his critique, so the power of cliché, though great, is not invincible, the system not entirely closed.

The particular piece of Snow's hackneyed wisdom upon which Leavis fastens at this point is the assertion that members of the scientific culture 'have the future in their bones', together with its companion claim that members of the 'traditional culture' are 'natural Luddites' (63–4). From the mid-nineteenth century, the use of this latter metaphor in English public debate involved a special kind of condescension. The original Luddites' outraged reaction to being displaced by machines may, it is implied, have been understandable and deserving of our sympathy, but their response was, 'at the end of the day', unrealistic: they could not arrest or divert the tide of economic progress. And thus, anyone who is described, metaphorically, as a 'Luddite' is being dismissed or, at the very least, patted on the head: by refusing to adapt to technological change they are merely parading their doomed unrealism. By trying to dig in their heels they are merely digging their own graves. In 'the real world', economic change happens; there's no point in bleating about it. ('Real' and its derivative forms occur with particular frequency in this discourse, indicating that a kind of ontological priority is being asserted.) Literary intellectuals are, according to Snow, 'natural Luddites'. Bleating about the costs of progress is what they do.

Snow had presented the contrast between the scientific and literary cultures as being in part about different responses to the industrial and technological revolutions. While the natural Luddites merely rail, the scientists get on with the business of improving the material conditions of life. The existence of the individual, Snow had added, expansively, ends in death and may therefore be considered tragic, but progress represents the onward sweep of humanity collectively: as individuals, 'each of us dies alone', but 'there is social hope'. Yet what, Leavis asks pressingly, 'is the "social hope" that transcends, cancels, or makes indifferent the inescapable tragic condition of each individual?' Where is such 'hope' to be found except in the lives lived by particular persons? And here Leavis makes one of his most characteristic argumentative moves: he cites D. H. Lawrence. Lawrence, 'the greatest English writer of our century', diagnosed the 'characteristic confusion' of the 'civilization of the West', above all in 'his supreme novel', *Women in Love*, which affirms that 'nothing matters but life'. This is proffered as a conclusive dismissal of Snow's airy invocation of 'social hope', but the reader may well feel that the form of the criticism involves preaching to the converted: no attempt is made to spell out *how* Lawrence's novel accomplishes this large task. Leavis elaborates his point by saying that Lawrence insists on 'the truth that only in living individuals is life there, and individual lives cannot be aggregated or equated or dealt with quantitatively in any way' (65–6). This objection appears to hover between banal ineffability and wild exaggeration. Where else *could* life be, and is it really true that 'living individuals' cannot be equated or dealt with quantitatively in *any* way? At first sight, this latter contention might seem to rule out all social science, indeed social data of any kind. But in affirming the Lawrentian maxim, Leavis is in reality training his sights elsewhere. The target is the implicit assumption that a social goal could be specified in aggregate terms, such as measures of a rising standard of living, without asking about the *quality* of the individual experiences that such measures presume to aggregate. Leavis's language at this point is almost a direct echo of Ruskin's famous maxim, used as part of a similar argument (against political economy, in his case): 'there is no wealth but life'.[12] In resorting to such language, Leavis and Ruskin (and others) come up against one of the recurring aporias of cultural criticism: quantitative or instrumental descriptions of the goals of life need

[12] John Ruskin, *Unto This Last* (1862), ed. Clive Wilmer (Harmondsworth: Penguin, 1985), p. 222.

to be shown up as inadequate and reductive, yet the character of the alternative ends up being merely gestured to by unsatisfactory phrases about 'life'.

Leavis's preferred strategy at this point (he resorts to it on many occasions in his cultural criticism) is to suggest that although an adequate characterization of the goals of human life cannot, without descending into vacuous abstraction, be given in propositional form, great novels can *embody* such a vision. They ask the question: 'What for – what ultimately for? What, ultimately, do men live by?' Leavis immediately and pre-emptively rules that 'Of course to such questions there can't be, in any ordinary sense of the word, "answers"' (68). In their place, and simply as a shorthand description of a more adequate conception of human life, Leavis points to the work of some of his cherished novelists, such as Conrad and, inevitably, Lawrence. In practice, he does little more than *name* one or two representative books: as so often with Leavis's literary judgements, their form implies that the work of discrimination has already been done and relative degrees of quality definitively established. Within the Richmond lecture he can legitimately suggest that the supporting evidence may be found elsewhere in his writings and those of other *Scrutiny* contributors. But the sufficiently interested reader who tries to pursue these judgements to their source can be left feeling that a kind of infinite regress is at work: even in Leavis's more extended literary-critical writings one can encounter the disconcerting sense that the real work of analysis had always already been performed, and that the reader is merely being issued with a reminder of what was 'plainly' the case.

In disputing the 'crass Wellsianism' of Snow's vision of the human future – more and more technological innovation and material prosperity – Leavis also takes issue with the interpretation of the past on which it rests. He singles out the following sentence as a particularly terrifying example of the 'callous' insensibility that passes for wisdom in Snow: 'For, with singular unanimity, in any country where they have had the chance, the poor have walked off the land into the factories as fast as the factories could take them.' This assertion was part of Snow's positive assessment of the Industrial Revolution, which formed in turn a central element in his larger commitment to a theory of progress. The application of technology to the betterment of the conditions of life was, he held, the central dynamic of human history. This process had speeded up immeasurably since the middle of the eighteenth century, and this had meant, for the mass of mankind, an almost immeasurable improvement in their conditions of life.

It is important, before going further, to be clear that Leavis was not denying the large element of truth in this historical story, nor was he suggesting that mankind should attempt to return to some version of pre-industrial existence – in itself an unintelligible as well as impracticable project. But he resists what he sees as Snow's reductively brisk characterization of the process – a process he finds to have been 'incomparably and poignantly more complex' – and he bridles at the dismissal of those who point to the human cost of these transformations as 'Luddities'. In other words, Leavis is trying to make room for questions about the 'lived quality' of the human lives which, collectively, constitute this historical process. And he particularly bridles at what he sees as Snow's explicit or tacit dismissal of the great critics of the human costs of industrialism from Dickens and Ruskin onwards. This is a vital affirmation of affiliation for Leavis. And it is important to him to make clear that this is by no means a reactionary tradition: he emphasizes the line running from Ruskin, down through Morris to British socialism and ultimately the welfare state. However, for these writers "'well-being" or "welfare" could not conceivably be matters of merely material standard of living'. The damaging emptiness of Snow's position, by contrast, is that he offers no more elaborated conception of human flourishing than the pursuit of yet more 'jam tomorrow'.

In contesting Snow's benignly optimistic interpretation of the consequences of the Industrial Revolution, as in his own related invocation of the more complex vision of the great novelists, Leavis is simultaneously pulling rank on Snow, by casting him in the role of superficial philistine, and bumping up against the limits of what cultural criticism can do by way of presenting a more adequate picture of human fulfilment. As so often, such criticism is carried by the adverbs more than by any other part of speech: these terms, perhaps characterizing the manner or tenor in which an idea is expressed, or helping to invoke common ground between critic and reader, serve to gesture towards – and, cumulatively, to start to constitute – a realm of recognized and assented-to judgements. It is by no means the case that all the leading cultural critics of the past century or more have been literary critics by primary profession, but the high frequency of the overlap is clearly not just a matter of chance or contingent social circumstance. Leavis may be expressing himself with distinctive pungency when he says of Snow's statements about the goal of more 'jam tomorrow': 'The callously ugly insensitiveness of the mode of expression is wholly significant' (71). But in general the use of more nuanced and delicately inflected language to show up the weaknesses of crass or formulaic writing is the stock-in-trade of the cultural critic.

Probably only a minority of its readers would describe the Richmond lecture as, in the words of one of its few admirers to enter the lists in the immediately ensuing furore, 'one of the greatest rhetorical performances I have ever read for mounting splendour of scornful irony',[13] but even those disposed to be reasonably sympathetic to Leavis's case would have to acknowledge a certain falling-off in its final pages, perhaps even a betraying misstep or two. Alarm bells begin to ring when Leavis (not Snow) glosses 'jam' as 'the prosperity and leisure enjoyed by our well-to-do working class'. The spectre of class condescension begins to hover; the shadow of the suggestion that while a high material standard of living may in the past have done no harm to the ruling or educated classes, it becomes toxic when extended to the majority, who are too uncultured to make 'proper' use of it. References to 'a vision of our imminent tomorrow in today's America' or to 'the human emptiness; emptiness and boredom craving alcohol' only increase the reader's unease. A prejudiced conservatism of a related kind is then suggested by Leavis's much quoted, and much derided, rhetorical question: 'Who will assert that the average member of a modern society is more fully human, or more alive, than

---

[13] G. S. Fraser, *Spectator* (16 March 1962), 333.

a Bushman, an Indian peasant, or a member of one of those poignantly surviving primitive peoples, with their marvellous art and skills and vital intelligence?' (72). That 'average member' suggests those eager but mindless consumers of 'jam' who belong to 'our well-to-do working class'; even the use of the possessive adjective can sound faintly patronizing here. And the poignancy attached to the lives of the 'Bushmen', 'peasants' and 'primitive peoples' seems, complicitly, more than a little wilful. It is certainly not obvious that the relentless struggle simply to stay alive that has been the historical lot of such people is humanly richer than the far more varied if in some ways unsatisfactory lives of those who live in prosperous modern societies. But whatever the truth of such a comparison – and it is hard to see how it could ever be worked through other than in the most gestural terms – Leavis's deployment of it at this point risks seeming tendentious and unconvincing.

And this danger is intensified when, in the closing paragraphs of the lecture, Leavis turns briefly to his understanding of the university as 'a centre of consciousness ... for our civilization'. His statement of this case begins promisingly with the observation that even the achievements of science depend upon the prior 'creation of the human world, including language' (74). This might point towards some examination of the ways in which all intellectual enquiry employs, and is embedded in, a thickly textured natural language whose creation is social and historical. But Leavis moves too quickly to what he presents as the corollary of his claim, namely that 'it is in the study of literature, the literature of one's own language in the first place, that one comes to recognize the nature and priority of the third realm' (his term for the elaborate edifice of culture that cannot be reduced either to the subjectively individual nor to the objectively empirical).[14] From this he moves no less quickly to the claim that the discipline of English must be at the heart of the university if that institution is really to be 'a centre of human consciousness'. And from that already exposed position he moves too quickly again to the assertion that the work that he and his fellow contributors to *Scrutiny* did exemplified the way in which 'a vital English School' should perform this function. On other occasions Leavis wrote at length about all these matters, but here the brevity and assertiveness of his case risked seeming the crassest kind of academic imperialism. They also, of course, laid him open to charges of self-importance, charges which the first wave of correspondents to the *Spectator* did not hesitate to press in robust terms.

But, buried in the provocative, self-referential prose of the final paragraphs were two asides which have perhaps not received the attention they deserve, and which bring the lecture back to its larger purpose. Having invoked his ideal of a 'vital English School', he goes on: 'I mustn't say more now about what I mean by that, I will only say that the academic is the enemy and that the academic *can* be beaten, as we who ran *Scrutiny* for twenty years proved'. And in expressing his hope that a Cambridge animated by such a centre of consciousness might become a place 'where the culture of the Sunday papers was not taken

---

[14] Leavis sketched his idea of 'the third realm' in 'Valuation in Criticism' (1966), reprinted in *Valuation in Criticism and Other Essays*, ed. G. Singh (Cambridge University Press, 1986), and in *The Living Principle: 'English' as a Discipline of Thought* (London: Chatto, 1975).

to represent the best that is thought and known in our time' (and where, as a result, it would be unnecessary to pay this amount of attention to Snow), he referred dismissively to 'the journalistic addiction of our academic intellectuals', adding 'and journalism (in one form or another) is now the menacing disease of university "English"' (75–7). At first sight, Leavis's antagonism both to the academic (meaning, I take it, a spirit or style of proceeding rather than the individual scholar) and the journalistic appears puzzling, even contradictory. These, it can sometimes seem, represent the two increasingly divergent camps in modern culture, two alternative literary protocols (as well as contrasting career paths) that between them are exhaustive of the available modes for comprehending and commenting upon the world. How can Leavis seem to be repudiating both of them? Where does that leave him to stand?

The answers to these questions help us identify the true character of Leavis's infamous attack on Snow. He believes that there is, potentially at least, a form of participation in public debate that is not in thrall to either of these dominant modes, and this is what he understands by 'the critical function'. All one's human and intellectual resources need to be mobilized to fully apprehend the facet of reality under examination, and all one's literary and persuasive capacities need to be deployed to make one's understanding vividly present for others. Such critical labour will eschew the vices of academicism – a sham impersonality, exaggerated deference to authorities, the avoidance of judgement – while at the same time avoiding the pitfalls characteristic of journalism – superficiality, sensationalism, attention-seeking, the over-valuing of what is merely topical or current. Such criticism will be outspoken, but also properly grounded. It will inevitably involve disputing the accepted wisdom and disparaging fashionable reputations. It will attempt to maintain the highest intellectual standards while constantly engaging in, rather than withdrawing from, public debate. It is this activity that Leavis intended his Richmond lecture to exemplify.

Responses and replies

Leavis's lecture, as noted above, provoked a small storm of correspondence and comment. It dominated the letters pages of the *Spectator* for several weeks, as well as being the subject of editorials and analyses there and elsewhere. Favourable or even-handed responses were almost drowned out by a chorus of condemnation. Leavis was held to be guilty of bad manners, bad faith and bad prose (this last was a common complaint throughout his career).[15] He was also held to be asserting the superiority of literature over science, of 'English' over other disciplines, of his own work above that of other critics. Nor were responses confined to the immediate context of publication, either temporally or geographically. The extended analysis of the episode by the American critic Lionel Trilling, quoted earlier, acquired a special status, and the reference in the subtitle of his article to 'the Leavis–Snow controversy' indicated what had soon become seen as the defining

---

[15] 'I know, of course, of the wide agreement that I write badly, but I don't think I'm commonly charged with lack of care to be precise'; letter to the *Spectator* (1963), reprinted in *Letters in Criticism by F. R. Leavis*, ed. John Tasker (London: Chatto, 1974), p. 106.

character of the topic.[16] When in 1964 two American academics thought the episode of sufficient importance to merit the compilation of a selection of contributions (and historical antecedents), they made it clear in their subtitle that the readings constituted 'Perspectives on the Snow–Leavis Controversy'.[17] And as Trilling drily noted, contributions to this controversy

were, with few exceptions, directed to such considerations as the exact degree of monstrousness which Dr Leavis achieved in speaking of Sir Charles as he did; whether or not he spoke out of envy of Sir Charles's reputation; whether or not he has, or deserves to have, any real standing as a critic; or writes acceptable English; or represents, as he claims he does, 'the essential Cambridge'.[18]

Leavis's response to the reception of the Richmond lecture, and his further elaboration of some of its themes, appeared in several disparate forms. The first, and briefest, came in the prefatory note he prefixed to the publication of his lecture as a separate volume by Chatto & Windus later in 1962. This opens combatively with the claim that 'The abundant adverse comment directed against my lecture hasn't advanced the argument by leaving me something to answer'. To the contrary, he took the largely hostile response to his lecture to have confirmed its analysis: 'The angry, abusive and strikingly confident utterances of Snow's supporters merely illustrated the nature

---

[16] See my introduction to Snow, *Two Cultures*, pp. xxxviii–xl.
[17] *Cultures in Conflict: Perspectives on the Snow—Leavis Controversy*, ed. David K. Cornelius and Edwin St Vincent (Chicago, IL: Scott, Foresman, 1964).
[18] Trilling, 'Science, literature, and culture', 463.

of the world or "culture" that had made Snow a mind, a sage, and a major novelist' (77). There is a logic to this claim, though it does raise the suspicion that *any* criticism or counterargument could be treated by Leavis as a symptom confirming his original diagnosis: wasn't this merely the dominant consensus closing ranks in the face of a discomfitingly accurate critique? The novel feature of Chatto's publication of the lecture was to accompany it with Yudkin's essay on Snow, reprinted from the *Cambridge Review*.[19] As noted earlier, Leavis had been eager to include this because it demonstrated that there were scientists who had reservations about Snow's case similar to his own. 'I feel it impossible to believe that scientists in considerable numbers will not acclaim Mr Yudkin's criticism of Snow as sound – and salutary.' Leavis doubtless hoped that pairing Yudkin's piece with his own would also help to dispel the misconception that his original critique rested on any kind of hostility to science and scientists.

The next occasion for further commentary was provided by the longer prefatory note that Leavis wrote for the American publication of his lecture in 1963. Here, he particularly took issue with Trilling's commentary on the episode. Trilling, as we have seen, roundly condemned Leavis's tone, the dismissive ferocity of his 'attack' on Snow. Far from acknowledging any justice in the charge, Leavis took it to indicate that even Trilling shared the values of the dominant elite ('even' because

[19] Almost fifty years later, Michael Yudkin recounted this episode in a paper delivered at the conference entitled 'Revaluing Leavis', which was held at Downing College, Cambridge, in 2009.

Trilling, perhaps America's most prominent literary critic at this point, shared so many interests and purposes with Leavis):

I have to comment that, in thus lending himself to the general cry that I have 'attacked' Snow (and 'attack' goes with the suggestion that I have indulged in an unpleasant display of personal animus), Professor Trilling, who passes as a vindicator of the critical function, seems to me guilty of *la trahison des clercs*. His attitude would make the essential work of the criticism today impossible. It belongs to the ethos I was intent on challenging. (79–80)

The calculated aggression of 'who passes as' surely risks alienating potential sympathizers here. Trilling's judicious (perhaps sometimes too self-consciously judicious) literary and cultural commentaries were renowned for their attempt to sustain the Arnoldian ideal of 'disinterestedness': if Trilling was not a 'vindicator of the critical function', then who was? The passage returns us again to the unsettling thought that Leavis regarded any response short of complete and enthusiastic agreement as a kind of 'treason' to the critical function. This suspicion is strengthened each time Leavis refers, as he does in this note, to the 'unanswerableness' of his case. What answer, then, could be acceptably made except abject acknowledgement of the complete truth of his every contention? He describes himself as aiming at a 'drastic finality' in his dismissal of Snow's stature. This describes the character of his critique well, if not modestly, but it also raises the disquieting suggestion that the very possibility of counter-argument is excluded. In expressing some sympathy with the indignation felt by Snow's supporters, Trilling stands condemned as betraying the cause of criticism. This seems to leave no room for responses which, while appreciating Leavis's central critical purpose, might wish to disown some of his more offensively *ad hominem* remarks. Leavis's reaction in this case makes it seem that it is simply not possible, in his ontology, to merit the title of 'critic' while expressing any reservations about the 'finality' of his case.

Leavis used the preface to the American edition as an occasion to rehearse a more general argument which he made elsewhere during these years (notably in his 'Retrospect' to the complete reissue of *Scrutiny* in 1963) about the lack of an effective 'educated public' in contemporary Britain. The facile, vogueish treatment of literary and cultural matters in the Sunday papers and smart weeklies demonstrated the point. In this croneyish, self-promoting world, no serious critical standards were in play, as they could not be, he maintained, where there was no public capable of making true discriminations of quality effective. And should a critic, from outside this coterie world, attempt to say that a whole succession of much lauded emperors in fact have no clothes, 'one finds arrayed against one a comprehensive system of personal relations' (82–3). Leavis has been much derided for the paranoid exaggeration of such claims, yet there was some truth to the suggestion (as there still is) that metropolitan literary culture rested on a series of overlapping social networks that were always likely to close ranks in the face of any sceptical external questioning of the system of reviewing and reputation-making.

Part, surely, of what is at issue both in Leavis's claim and the literary world's response is a clash of discursive fields and their underlying social frameworks. Leavis writes as someone who is defiantly not part of metropolitan literary culture, yet he presumes to pass judgement on it and its valuations. For the most part, the metropolitan literary culture has no difficulty either with academics who confine themselves to academic scholarship, with its corresponding forms of professional publication, or with those few academics who accede to the protocols of 'trade' publishing and become regular Sunday reviewers. But it finds something offensive in the idea of a university-based critic invoking more strenuous and probing standards with which not just to challenge the conventional estimations of certain highly touted writers or books, but to arraign the system which produces such shallow judgements. Leavis's later career, and the reactions he provoked, can be seen as an extended commentary on the dynamic of this interaction between discordant discursive worlds. He perceived the extent to which the literary world is an endogenous system which believes that, through the mechanism of the market, it is responding to the tastes of a reading public when in fact, as he trenchantly puts it, 'the "literary world" is its own public'. In other words, the operative standards that govern success and failure in trade publishing are not directly given by some amorphous power called 'public taste', but by the conventional wisdom among the self-reinforcing ranks of publishers, editors, reviewers, agents, publicists and so on about what that taste 'wants' or will tolerate. Leavis's observation about that world retains its purchase and its relevance: 'It hates the suggestion that there might be another, one to be feared: a real educated public that doesn't take the "literary world" seriously' (85). In the context of ruminations on the reception of his Richmond lecture, these comments were bound to seem self-serving, but that is not sufficient reason to dismiss them simply as paranoid ravings.

'Luddites?'

The principal occasion for returning to these themes was provided by the lecture entitled 'Luddites? or There is only one culture' which Leavis gave at Cornell and Harvard universities in 1966, and then published, first in the 1969 volume *Lectures in America* (jointly with Q. D. Leavis), and then in the 1972 volume *Nor Shall My Sword*. In its relation to the Richmond lecture, this piece in some respects parallels the relation of Snow's 'Second Look' to his Rede Lecture, and it is included in the present volume as Snow's later piece was included in the matching Canto edition of his lecture.

'I am used to being misrepresented, but not resigned to it.' His opening sentence is again arresting, not just signalling his view of the bulk of the responses to his Richmond lecture, but also immediately drawing attention to the matter of his own reputation, or supposed reputation. Nor does he hesitate to stress that this is part of a systemic problem: anyone who has taken a line at all similar to his knows 'how gross and inconsequent is the misrepresentation that follows, and how impossible it is to get the case one has put attended to' (89). The use of 'impossible' may cause the reader to stiffen a little: Leavis's position already threatens to be both self-confirming and invulnerable. One might have thought that, by any measure, Leavis's lecture had been 'attended to'; few pieces of writing are made the subject of such a volume of commentary and response. But he is insisting that the 'case' he had put had not been attended to because the responses had focussed overmuch on his alleged failings of tone and breaches of the etiquette of public debate, though once again it is hard to suppress the suspicion that only complete agreement would count for Leavis as properly 'attending to' his case.

'Luddites?', it should be acknowledged at the outset, does not have the sustained rhetorical power of the Richmond lecture, in part because it involves a series of skirmishes with several different antagonists. But in dwelling on questions about the quality of human life as a series of challenges to the contemporary over-valuation of economic prosperity as an end in itself, he retrospectively highlights the true theme of the earlier lecture. There is no discussion here of science 'versus' the humanities, or of the priority of one over the other in educational arrangements, or indeed of most of the issues with which 'two cultures' talk has come to be associated. Leavis's focus is not on the actual character of intellectual disciplines, but on what the whole discourse *around* the idea of 'the two cultures' – initially as articulated by Snow but then as respectfully repeated by others – tells us about the state of contemporary 'civilization'. And, as his title indicates, his entry point is the use of 'Luddite' to castigate anyone who appears to express the slightest reservation about economic growth as a self-sufficient social ideal, and how this move forecloses the possibility of discussing the substantive theme.

A point recurrently at issue between Leavis and his critics concerned his alleged nostalgia. Did he regret the material progress of the past two hundred years and was he recommending that we should, to the extent that such a recommendation could be intelligible, 'return' to some kind of preindustrial way of life? Leavis makes it as plain as he can that he holds neither of these views. What he is urging is that, as part of a proper concern with the possibilities of human life in the machine age, we should have some vivid apprehension of what has been lost as well as what has been gained as a result of technological change. His focus is, unswervingly, the present, but he is intent on combatting what he sees as the wilful amnesia that cuts us off from any understanding of the true character of life in previous ages. And he insists, even more disputably, that literature provides uniquely powerful access to that life. 'It is the great novelists above all who give us our social history; compared with what is done in *their* work – their creative work – the histories of the professional social historian seem empty and unenlightening' (93). This is one of those places where Leavis needlessly gives hostages to fortune. It is not necessary, in order to validate the distinctive imaginative power with which the novel may illuminate the lived experience of the past, to appear to dismiss social historians, whose purposes and methods are inevitably and properly rather different. This made it easier for J. H. Plumb and other historians marshalled in support of Snow to suggest that Leavis was disregarding the weight of historical scholarship on the social consequences of the Industrial Revolution, just as his incautious celebration of the skills and satisfactions of the craftsmen of earlier centuries laid him open to repeated jibes about his one-eyed attachment to 'the old wheelwright's shop'.[20]

---

[20] Such criticisms were not left to chance, but were carefully orchestrated by Snow and Plumb: 'We must smash the influence of this man – as

In moving to give some account of the positive alternative he is proposing to the prevailing economism, Leavis repeatedly registers the impossibility of providing precise definitions where the ends of human life are concerned. 'I won't proceed by attempting to offer a direct formal definition' is the guiding note of his discussion. The work of science, he repeats, is dependent upon 'a prior human achievement . . . the creation of the human world, including language'. It is important that this truth be 'given full conscious realizing recognition', yet it seems impossible to obtain more than 'a mere notional assent' to it. He quotes from a leading article in the *Guardian* which concluded, in a phrase that might have seemed to concede much of Leavis's case: 'Science is a means to an end'. His response is indicative of what 'full conscious realizing recognition' might be like. The *Guardian*'s proposition is true, but it risks turning into a truism: the point is made too easily. It lacks any of 'the friction, the sense of pregnant arrest, which goes with active realizing thought and the taking of a real charged meaning' (103). The unsympathetic reader may feel that this amounts to little more than the demand that others write in the same kind of sinuous, qualification-packed prose as Leavis, but that may be to miss his deeper point. Leavis is suggesting that we do not best combat one reductive truism by proposing a different one in its place: in trying to gesture towards more

remorselessly as we can', as Plumb put it, and on another occasion he proudly reported to Snow that his article 'Progress and the Historians' 'finishes with a flaming attack on Leavis and all his works'; letters 1.7.62 and 9.9.63 (C. P. Snow papers, Harry Ransom Humanities Center, Austin, Texas). For 'the wheelwright's shop' jibes, see note 7 below.

adequate conceptions of human ends, a prose which displays 'the friction, the sense of pregnant arrest' characteristic of 'active realizing thought' *is itself part of the answer*. Over and over again, Leavis introduces this kind of arrest into his writing, questioning even the terms, especially the terms, that seem most naturally to come to hand when articulating an alternative vision. It is easy to say that human ends transcend the pursuit of a 'rising standard of living', but this summative citation of 'ends'

tends, perhaps, to turn the receptivity of the mind away from orders of consideration that are essential – essential, that is, when the criteria for determining how we should discriminate and judge in the face of a rapidly changing civilization are what we want to bring to full consciousness. (104)

As so often, his much complained-about prose was here attempting to enact the mind's struggle to reach towards a perspective on life that defies easy description. Similarly, it can readily be said, in criticizing the emptiness of merely economic aims, that human beings need to find life 'significant', but that is to say very little. 'If, of course, one is challenged to stand and deliver and say what "significance" is – "If you use the term you ought to be able to say what you mean by it" – it is hardly possible to answer convincingly at the level of the challenge.' 'At the level of the challenge': here Leavis is acknowledging the requirements, but also the limitations, of public debate. It is not possible in that setting to respond with a brief and decisive formulation that won't thereby betray the larger case one is trying to make. So, where to turn for assistance? In considering the question of human ends, 'one's thinking should not be blind to the insights given in cultural tradition'.

But before pursuing this thought, Leavis inserts his hall-mark meta-commentary: 'This is not a simple answer; no serious answer *could* be.' By thus constantly intruding the second-order questions about the status of any attempt at first-order statement, Leavis is deliberately calling attention to the inherent difficulties of the enterprise. This is not a defensive twitch or an excess of self-consciousness: it *is* his reply.

Insofar as 'Luddites?' points towards any practical or institutional embodiment of an alternative perspective, it points, once again, to the university and, within that, to an 'English School' as a kind of 'liaison centre'. But in response to a comment by a well-meaning supporter that Leavis evidently hoped 'literary criticism will save us',[21] he made his celebrated declaration: 'I don't believe in any "literary values", and you won't find me talking about them; the judgements the literary critic is concerned with are judgements about life' (110). Leavis did not believe himself to be advocating some kind of 'literarism' (Aldous Huxley's term for his position) as a counterweight to Snow's scientism. He believed, with urgent intensity, that he was calling attention to fundamental, if not easily statable, questions about the *quality* of human experience, and that the kind of attentiveness and responsiveness inculcated by properly rigorous literary criticism – a discipline which, as he repeatedly insisted elsewhere, trained 'intelligence and sensibility together'[22] – had a vital role

---

[21] See note 13 below.
[22] See, for a frequently cited instance, F. R. Leavis, *Education and the University: A Sketch for an 'English School'* (London: Chatto, 1943), pp. 34–5: English 'trains, in a way no other discipline can, intelligence and sensibility together'.

to play in helping to combat the numbness and inattention fostered by accelerated technological change. Only if it played that role, outside the university as well as in, was there any hope of nurturing 'an effective educated public', which could then in turn be expected to distinguish between serious thinking about human ends and the vacuous official platitudes peddled by those 'publicizers, public relations men, heads of houses, academic ward-bosses, hobnobbers with Cabinet ministers' whom he believed betrayed the true function of his own university (111).

Leavis thus ends, as he had begun, with Cambridge, thereby inviting charges of parochialism and obsessive grievance. But it had been in Cambridge that Snow had delivered his original lecture, and it was to the true Cambridge that Leavis looked for a properly critical response to it – that Cambridge of the mind which was, for him, a star to guide by as well as the land of lost content. If there was to be a centre of resistance to 'the blind enlightened menace' represented by Snow and the wider endorsement of his empty sermonizing, then it would have to be found in universities; economic and technological change had rendered the effective functioning of an educated public in the wider society impossible. And even the universities were, in Leavis's eyes, now under threat from ill-considered expansion. Lord Robbins, symbolically if not practically the chief architect of this expansion, figured prominently in Leavis's demonology in the 1960s, especially for the priority he appeared to give (in his famous report on higher education) to meeting 'the needs of the economy'.[23] Leavis saw both Robbins and Snow as

[23] Lionel Robbins, one of the leading economists of his generation as well as a major public figure, had chaired the independent committee

symptoms of a deeper malaise, and he is wholly unsurprised to find Robbins, in affecting astonishment at the 'very high passions' aroused by Snow's lecture, saying: 'To me his diagnosis seems obvious'. But *that*, as Leavis does not have to spell out, is the heart of the problem, and his own final words are unyielding; 'To me it seems obvious that Snow's *raison d'être* is to be an elementary test' (112).

Snow made no public comment on the Richmond lecture until after the publication in 1970 of Leavis's essay 'Literarism versus scientism: the misconception and the menace'.[24] Even then, Snow's article 'The case of Leavis and the serious case' did not attempt to respond directly to any of the main criticisms.[25] Instead, it complained that Leavis did not follow the basic ground rules of intellectual exchange as far as factual truth and accurate quotation were concerned and so no fruitful discussion could take place. It is understandable that Snow did not want to enter into debate about the nature of his reputation or the merits of his own work, but this somewhat dismissive tactic also meant that he offered no response on the substantive matters such as the relative standing of the goal of

which in its 1963 report had recommended a substantial expansion of higher education in Britain; see the discussion in John Carswell, *Government and the Universities in Britain: Programme and Performance 1960–1980* (Cambridge University Press, 1985).

[24] This essay, which dealt with the broader issues of the cultural role of technology (including computers) and the expansion of the universities, only touched on Snow in passing. It was first published in the *Times Literary Supplement* in April 1970, then reprinted in *Nor Shall My Sword: Discourses on Pluralism, Compassion and Social Hope* (London: Chatto & Windus, 1972), pp. 137–60.

[25] First published in the *Times Literary Supplement* in July 1970, and reprinted in *Public Affairs*, pp. 81–98.

economic prosperity. It is more curious that although he charged Leavis with 'inaccurate quotations, wrong attributions, and incorrect biographical innuendoes', the evidence he provided to support these charges should seem so flimsy.

Snow's handling of the charge of misquotation illustrates the point. He claimed that the Richmond lecture included 'approximately twenty' passages quoted from his Rede lecture: 'Of these, something under half are false – that is, the words he uses are not the words I wrote', adding 'Some of these misquotations are comparatively trivial: others distort and garble the meaning'.[26] But perhaps Snow was himself being less than wholly accurate here. By my count, there are twenty-two passages in the Richmond lecture which are presented as quotations from Snow's text. Thirteen of them are quoted exactly. Seven others have insignificant or acceptable errors or alterations in them: insignificant as in the omission of a comma or addition of a hyphen, acceptable as in replacing 'the scientists' with 'they' to maintain the structure of a sentence when quoted. None of these affect the sense or tone at all. There remain two which could be thought of as culpable misquotation. In the first, Leavis renders Snow's phrase 'each of us dies alone' as 'we die alone', which arguably tends, at least tonally, to smudge the contrast between the individual and the group which was at the heart of Snow's point. And in the second, where Snow is talking of the process of industrialization in Russia and China and says 'The transformations have also proved something which only the scientific culture can take in its stride', Leavis

[26] Snow, *Public Affairs*, p. 81.

misquotes 'proved' as 'provided'. Only in this case could it be argued that the error 'garbles the meaning'. Misquotation is, of course, a serious fault and potentially a damaging one when a critic is laying such stress on the poverty of an opponent's language. But Snow's faux-statistical way of reporting Leavis's transgressions may be thought to be more misleading than any of the minor errors themselves.

It is often assumed that the proper outcome of a polemical public exchange should be a removal of misunderstandings and a narrowing of the area of disagreement. It can hardly be said that the so-called 'Snow–Leavis debate' conformed to this model. But as one ponders the statements and restatements of the respective cases, it becomes increasingly hard to imagine either of the main protagonists yielding any ground. Snow (and the many correspondents and commentators who took his side) regarded Leavis as utterly incapable of understanding why his critique might have been misconceived or unacceptable: in their eyes, the only sufficient indication that he had appreciated the force and justice of the objections made to his attack would have been an improbable *mea culpa* acknowledging that his criticisms of Snow were unwarranted and his analysis of the way the dominant consensus functioned was unfounded. Conversely, for Leavis (and his much smaller number of supporters), it could seem that the only acceptable indication that his charges had been properly apprehended and pondered would have been a declaration by his critics that Snow had no claim on the standing he had hitherto been accorded, that this standing was indeed a symptom of a corrupt and unthinking public realm, and that, yes, material prosperity had been treated as axiomatically the goal of human endeavour but that Leavis had alerted readers to the poverty of this conception. It is difficult, as I've already suggested, to imagine Leavis regarding a response short of such abject surrender as anything but confirmation of his original analysis. The metaphor of ships in the night hardly does justice to the gulfs between the main protagonists in what Leavis was right to say could not properly be called a 'debate'.

The challenge of cultural criticism

Perhaps few if any readers, then or now, would consider that all the parts of Leavis's analysis were equally well judged. Even allowing for the genre (on which more below), there are features of his critique which, for many readers, still seem gratuitous and thus risk being counterproductive. But while Leavis's tactics may occasionally have misfired or been disproportionate, his strategy is worth reflecting on, since it was a bold attempt to confront some of the enduring challenges and dilemmas of cultural criticism.

The first of these is how to find both a platform and a mode of expression that will ensure that views which are dissident or critical of widely shared assumptions get a proper hearing. Leavis may have over-dramatized his 'exclusion': in this later part of his career, at least, he rarely seems to have had much difficulty in placing an article in one of the mainstream periodicals when he chose to do so.[27] Nonetheless, we can give a sharper edge to the

[27] See Stefan Collini, 'The critic as anti-journalist: Leavis after *Scrutiny*', in *Grub Street and the Ivory Tower: Literary Journalism and Literary Scholarship from Fielding to the Internet*, ed. Jeremy Treglown and Bridget Bennett (Oxford University Press, 1998), pp. 151–76.

question by imagining some (actually highly improbable) counterfactual possibilities. Let us suppose that Leavis had brought out a carefully detailed analysis of Snow's fiction in a strictly scholarly journal such as the *Review of English Studies*, or let us imagine that he had published a brief, well-informed disagreement with Snow's educational views in the *Times Educational Supplement*. Some readers may feel that these would have been more practical – or, in the current weasel phrase, 'more helpful' – responses, but there can be no doubt that they would have received far less attention. Moreover, the cautious statement of limited disagreements with Snow would, far from calling his standing as a sage into question, have indirectly reinforced that standing. In such cases, it is the whole mechanism by which celebrity is transmuted into authority that needs to be exposed. It is hard to see how this can be done without giving offence to those who themselves have colluded with or been the beneficiaries of that process. And if it is not simply one or other *particular* view that requires to be criticized, but the poverty of mind that finds expression in such inadequate views more generally, then there may be no more telling mode than astringent literary criticism. As I hinted earlier, simply holding up a sample of the objectionable prose in the tweezers of quotation can sometimes be one of the most deadly ways to call attention to the crippling or embarrassing inadequacy of the underlying view of the world. Such critical tactics always risk seeming condescending or sneering, but that may be a risk the cultural critic has to take if the systemic limitations of the perspective under examination are to be properly exposed.

Leavis had long been aware of this logic and had conducted his 'field performances' accordingly.[28] Both the character and purpose of his forays into public debate in these years came more clearly into focus when the Richmond lecture was reprinted, alongside 'Luddites?' and four other pieces in the 1972 volume *Nor Shall My Sword*. In this form, it fell into place as one of several attempts to undermine the self-evidence of those 'enlightened orthodoxies' which, according to Leavis, dominated metropolitan opinion and its favoured media outlets – the Sunday papers, the smart weeklies, the BBC, the British Council and so on (the litany became wearyingly familiar as Leavis's attacks multiplied). He sardonically referred to these forays as 'the higher pamphleteering', but he clearly gave much thought to the occasions and form of his interventions.[29] When bringing these pieces together as the volume *Nor Shall My Sword*, he wrote to one correspondent: 'I remember having told someone myself that the Richmond Lecture is a poem. "Musically organized" is what I've also said about my lectures – the necessity of making each of which self-contained helped me to conceive the book – helped me to solve the greater writing (*thinking*) problem.'[30] Whether or not we are prepared to grant Leavis his metaphors here – to some, the 'music' still seems deliberately discordant and rebarbative – we have to recognize that the tone and address of these pieces were consciously chosen and crafted, not the uncontrolled thrashing of blind rage.

[28] For his 'field performances' (Leavis's own term), see MacKillop, *Leavis*, p. 375.

[29] See ibid., pp. 374–5. [30] Quoted ibid., p. 328.

Since Leavis's lecture provoked so many hostile or dismissive responses, it is clearly pertinent to ask in what sense his literary tactics could be regarded as successful. Were his critics right that the tone and angle of address of Leavis's lecture were self-defeating – that, far from discrediting Snow and what he represented, he only succeeded in discrediting himself? This question also has a more general application. Whenever a critic departs from the prevailing norms of public discussion – whether by being deliberately provocative, or by appearing to be hopelessly unrealistic or intransigent, or by using the weapons of satire or humour, or by any other way of disturbing the discursive equilibrium – s/he is likely to be reproved for sacrificing the possibility of making a 'positive' and 'constructive' contribution to debate to the satisfactions of self-expressive or self-indulgent display. But what if the critic believes that the categories and assumptions involved in any contribution that might be regarded as 'constructive' by the prevailing consensus are precisely what need to be challenged? And what if, further, the critic is right to think that s/he will never succeed in gaining attention for any alternative framework, still less assent to it, except by infringing the conventional decorum of discussion in some way? Such considerations raise, in turn, even more fundamental questions about what is to count as 'success' when contributing to public debate.

As usual, one effect of deliberate outspokenness was to have given voice to a view which others already held in partial or embryonic form, thus emboldening them also to speak out publicly. One reader wrote to the *Spectator* to say 'how grateful some of my colleagues in adult education and I feel for the publication of the Richmond lecture', since they found 'Dr Leavis's strictures on C. P. Snow and on the society that takes him so seriously are entirely justified, self-evident, and life-enhancing'.[31] Another declared: 'It is surely only just to admit the basic truth of Leavis's criticism of Snow's work as a novelist and popularizer of ideas'. The indignation in the letters defending Snow was 'merely an indication that Leavis has hit his target. One wonders why the attack has been so long delayed.'[32] In similar vein, Charles Raven, the former Master of Christ's (who, admittedly, had reason not to admire his onetime colleague's fictional account of college life) wrote to thank Leavis for having had 'the courage to say what some of us ought to have said long ago'.[33] In judging the 'success' of a piece of cultural criticism, we should not confine ourselves to a simplistic model of 'converting' one's opponents. Such writing may reach several publics, and we need to consider also such categories as fortifying, reassuring, giving voice to, helping to articulate, redirecting attention, and so on. Nor should we think only of the immediate reactions; any number of works have gone on to have considerable standing and influence despite initially being met with hostile responses and reviews. But even when all this has been said, many readers may still be unwilling to regard Leavis's lecture as any kind of 'success': offensiveness of this order is not soon forgiven.

There may be no way of assessing whether Leavis's critique affected Snow's standing and cultural authority. Indeed, it could be said that since the apogee of Snow's

[31] Letter by G. N. A. Guinness, *Spectator* (23 March 1962), 367.
[32] Letter from J. F. L. Long, *Spectator* (23 March 1962), 367.
[33] Quoted in MacKillop, *Leavis*, p. 322.

public career – his brief spell as a minister in Harold Wilson's 1964 government – came soon after Leavis's attack, he cannot have done any significant damage. On the other hand, Snow himself, an inveterate gong hunter with no low estimation of his own achievements, seems to have believed that the assault jeopardized his chances of the Nobel Prize for literature.[34] He certainly remained in demand as a public speaker and commentator throughout the 1960s, though sales of his novels began to fall off. It is probably fair to say that the reputations of both Snow and Leavis dipped in their final years and declined immediately after their deaths (in 1980 and 1978 respectively). While Snow's has never revived (despite the continuing attention given to the idea of 'the two cultures'), there has been in recent years a substantial amount of serious interest in Leavis's work, including his late forays into public debate.[35]

The attempt to articulate, in such a forum, an alternative to reductive instrumentalism involves a familiar tension or paradox. Most forms of public debate demand brevity and punchiness, but brevity and punchiness encourage reductivism. The critic of the instrumentalism of treating

[34] See Snow to Plumb, 7 March 1962 (J. H. Plumb papers, Cambridge University Library); see also Philip A. Snow, *Stranger and Brother: A Portrait of C. P. Snow* (London: Macmillan, 1982), p. 130.

[35] There have, however, been attempts to revive interest in Snow as a novelist as well as a public figure: see, for example, David Cannadine, 'C. P. Snow, "The Two Cultures", and the "Corridors of Power" revisited', in *Yet More Adventures with Britannia*, ed. Wm. Roger Louis (London: I. B. Tauris, 2005), and, most recently, Nicolas Tredell, *C. P. Snow: The Dynamics of Hope* (London: Palgrave, 2012). For examples of the more extensive scholarly discussion of Leavis, see A Note on Further Reading below, especially Bell, MacKillop, Storer and Ortolano.

increased economic prosperity as the overriding goal will always, in effect, be asking what, in turn, prosperity itself is good for. But that is to set oneself up to give some description of the ends of life. 'What for – what ultimately for? What, ultimately, do men live by?' A parade of abstract nouns has limited value as an answer. Implying an alternative vision, infiltrating it into the critique of one's opponent's language, may be the only strategy for avoiding such vacuity. There is rarely any shortage of suitable targets. The leaden, cliché-ridden, over-abstraction of so many official documents; the slack, fashion-driven chatter of so much journalism; the meaningless hype of almost all advertising and marketing; the coercive tendentiousness of all that worldly-wise, at-the-end-of-the-day, pronouncing – against these formidable social forces the critic goes into battle armed with little more than a closer attentiveness to the ways words mean and mislead, express truths and obstruct communication, stir the imagination and anaesthetize the mind.

But perhaps, as I have already suggested, we should recognize that the very process of such criticism *is* the alternative to brisk explicit statement. Or maybe what is needed, by analogy with the 'slow food' movement, is acknowledgement of the role of 'slow criticism', which, by its indirection and arrest, causes readers to lose their habitually confident footing and to stumble into more probing or reflective thinking. This does not entirely liberate the critic from the discursively awkward position of appearing to speak on behalf of the ineffable. But by drawing attention to the *critical engagement itself*, it starts the insidious process by which a prevailing discourse comes to seem shallow or misleading or in some other way inadequate.

From one point of view, Leavis might not seem an obvious recruit to any putative 'slow criticism' movement. As he himself wryly notes, one Italian periodical described him as '*puritano frenetico*',[36] and the intense, combative address of his printed voice does not at first conjure up the process by which the patient accretion of alternative descriptions, almost geological in the pace of its operation, modifies existing sensibilities. Anger operates at a faster tempo, and the Richmond lecture is a deeply angry performance. But closer familiarity with his much-remarked syntax suggests that it should be seen as, precisely, a straining against the limits of sequential exposition in the interests of recognizing the simultaneity and interrelatedness of considerations that are flattened by others into blandly self-contained propositions, which in turn congeal into cliché. To be disturbed into an awareness (however uneasy or resistant) of this process is to start to register the power of his critical voice. In these terms, perhaps Leavis's lecture, whatever its flaws, may still be thought to have a claim on our attention, even if opinion remains divided over whether it should be considered a minor classic of cultural criticism.

[36] Introduction to *Nor Shall My Sword*, p. 30.

49

A note on further reading

The indispensable bibliography of writings by and about F. R. and Q. D. Leavis (up to 1984) is M. B. Kinch, William Baker and John Kimber, *F. R. Leavis and Q. D. Leavis: An Annotated Bibliography* (New York: Garland, 1989). The standard biography is Ian MacKillop, *F. R. Leavis: A Life in Criticism* (London: Allen Lane, 1995). This may be supplemented by Denys Thompson, ed., *The Leavises: Recollections and Impressions* (Cambridge University Press, 1984), and 'F. R. Leavis Special Issue: Reminiscences and Revaluations', *Cambridge Quarterly* 25 (1996). The best introduction to Leavis's work is Michael Bell, *F. R. Leavis* (London: Routledge, 1988). A good recent brief account is Richard Storer, *F. R. Leavis* (London: Routledge, 2009). For works by and on C. P. Snow, see the note on further reading in my Canto edition of Snow's *Two Cultures* (Cambridge University Press, 1993); for references to more recent discussions of Snow, see Nicolas Tredell, *C. P. Snow: The Dynamics of Hope* (London: I. B. Tauris, 2012).

Several of the contributions to the 'Snow–Leavis debate' were collected in *Cultures in Conflict; Perspectives on the Snow–Leavis Controversy*, ed. David K. Cornelius and Edwin St Vincent (Chicago, IL: Scott, Foresman, 1964). For an excellent and fully documented discussion of the 'two cultures' theme and its place in British culture, see Guy Ortolano, *The Two Cultures Controversy: Science, Literature, and Cultural Politics in Postwar Britain* (Cambridge University Press, 2009).

A note on the text

As I explained in the Introduction above, Leavis's Richmond lecture was published in more than one form. It initially appeared in the *Spectator*, 9 March 1962, pages 297 to 303. The main title was given as 'The significance of C. P. Snow', with a smaller heading 'The Two Cultures?'. The following week the *Spectator* published a letter from Leavis (page 335) providing several corrections to the text as printed (though he did not refer to the heading given to the article). In October of that year the lecture was published as *Two Cultures? The Significance of C. P. Snow*, 'Being the Richmond Lecture, 1962. With an essay on Sir Charles Snow's Rede Lecture, by Michael Yudkin' (London: Chatto & Windus, 1962). In 1963 it was published in the USA by Pantheon Books, New York, 'with a new preface for the American reader'. It was then reprinted under the title 'Two Cultures? The Significance of Lord Snow', in F. R. Leavis, *Nor Shall My Sword: Discourses on Pluralism, Compassion and Social Hope* (London: Chatto & Windus, 1972).

'Luddites? Or, there is only one culture' was delivered as a lecture in the USA in 1966 and then published in F. R. and Q. D. Leavis, *Lectures in America* (London: Chatto & Windus, 1969). It was reprinted in *Nor Shall My Sword* in 1972.

The texts of the present edition are taken from *Nor Shall My Sword*, the last versions to be published in Leavis's lifetime, except that in the title of the Richmond lecture 'C. P. Snow' has been reinstated in place of 'Lord Snow'. There are otherwise no significant variants between these versions and those published by Chatto in 1962 and 1969 respectively.

Two Cultures?
The Significance of C. P. Snow (1962)

~

If confidence in oneself as a master-mind, qualified by capacity, insight and knowledge to pronounce authoritatively on the frightening problems of our civilization, is genius, then there can be no doubt about Sir Charles Snow's. He has no hesitations. Of course, anyone who offers to speak with inwardness and authority on both science and literature will be conscious of more than ordinary powers, but one can imagine such consciousness going with a certain modesty – with a strong sense, indeed, of a limited range and a limited warrant. The peculiar quality of Snow's assurance expresses itself in a pervasive tone; a tone of which one can say that, while only genius could justify it, one cannot readily think of genius adopting it. It is the tone we have (in so far as it can be given in an isolated sentence) here:

The only writer of world-class who seems to have had an understanding of the industrial revolution was Ibsen in his old age: and there wasn't much that old man didn't understand.

Clearly, there is still less Sir Charles Snow doesn't understand: he pays the tribute with authority. We take the implication and take it more surely at its full value because it carries the *élan*, the essential inspiration, of the whole self-assured performance. Yet Snow is in fact portentously ignorant. No doubt he could himself pass with ease the tests he proposes for his literary friends with the intimation that *they* would fail them, and so expose themselves as deplorably less well educated in respect of science than he, though a scientist, can claim to be in respect of literature. I have no doubt that *he* can define a machine-tool and state the second law of thermodynamics.[1] It is even possible, I suppose (though I am obliged to say that the evidence seems to me to be against it), that he could make a plausible show of being inward with the Contradiction of Parity, that esoteric upshot of highly subtle experiment which, he suggests, if things were well with our education, would have been a major topic at our High Tables. But of history, of the nature of civilization and of the history of its recent developments, of the human history of the Industrial Revolution, of the human significances entailed in that revolution, of literature, of the nature of that kind of collaborative human creativity of which literature is the type, it is hardly an exaggeration to say that Snow exposes complacently a complete ignorance.

The judgment I have to come out with is that not only is he not a genius; he is intellectually as undistinguished as it is possible to be. If that were all, and Snow were merely negligible, there would be no need to say so in any insistent public way, and one wouldn't choose to do it. But I used the adverb 'portentously' just now with full intention: Snow is a portent. He is a portent in that, being in himself negligible, he has become for a vast public on both sides of the Atlantic a master-mind and a sage. His significance is that he has been accepted – or perhaps the point is better made by saying 'created': he has been created as authoritative intellect by the cultural conditions manifested in his acceptance. Really distinguished minds are themselves, of course, *of* their age; they are responsive at the deepest level

54

to its peculiar strains and challenges: that is why they are able to be truly illuminating and prophetic and to influence the world positively and creatively. Snow's relation to the age is of a different kind; it is characterized not by insight and spiritual energy, but by blindness, unconsciousness and automatism. He doesn't know what he means, and doesn't know he doesn't know. That is what his intoxicating sense of a message and a public function, his inspiration, amounts to. It is not any challenge he thinks of himself as uttering, but the challenge he *is*, that demands our attention. The commentary I have to make on him is necessarily drastic and dismissive; but don't, I beg, suppose that I am enjoying a slaughterous field-day. Snow, I repeat, is in himself negligible. My preoccupation is positive in spirit. Snow points to its nature when he turns his wisdom upon education and the university.

I have not been quick to propose for myself the duty of dealing with him: that will, I hope, be granted. *The Two Cultures and the Scientific Revolution*, the Rede lecture which established him as an Intellect and a Sage, was given at this ancient university in 1959. I turned over the pages of the printed lecture in the show-room of the Cambridge University Press, was struck by the mode of expression Snow found proper and natural, perceived plainly enough what kind of performance the lecture was, and had no inclination to lay down three and sixpence. To my surprise, however, it rapidly took on the standing of a classic. It was continually being referred to – and not only in the Sunday papers – as if Snow, that rarely qualified and profoundly original mind, had given trenchant formulation to a key contemporary truth. What brought me to see that I must overcome the inner protest, and pay my three and sixpence, was the realizing, from marking scholarship scripts, that sixth-form masters were making their bright boys read Snow as doctrinal, definitive and formative – and a good examination investment.[2]

Well, I bought the lecture last summer, and, having noted that it had reached the sixth printing, read it through. I was then for the first time in a position to know how mild a statement it is to say that *The Two Cultures* exhibits an utter lack of intellectual distinction and an embarrassing vulgarity of style. The lecture, in fact, with its show of giving us the easily controlled spontaneity of the great man's talk, exemplifies kinds of bad writing in such richness and so significant a way that there would, I grant, be some point in the schoolmaster's using it as a text for elementary criticism; criticism of the style, here, becomes, as it follows down into analysis, criticism of the thought, the essence, the pretensions.

The intellectual nullity is what constitutes any difficulty there may be in dealing with Snow's panoptic pseudocogencies, his parade of a thesis: a mind to be argued with – that is not there; what we have is something other. Take that crucial term 'culture', without which and the work he relies on it to do for him Snow would be deprived of his seer's profundity and his show of a message. His use of it focuses for us (if I may be permitted what seems to me an apt paradox) the intellectual nullity; it confronts us unmistakably with the absence of the thought that is capable of posing problems (let alone answering them). The general nature of his position and his claim to authority are well known: there are the two uncommunicating and mutually indifferent cultures, there is the need to bring them together, and there is C. P. Snow, whose place in history is that he has them both, so that we have in him the paradigm of the desired and necessary union.

Snow is, of course, a – no, I can't say that; he isn't; Snow thinks of himself as a novelist. I don't want to discuss that aspect of him, but I can't avoid saying something. The widespread belief that he is a distinguished novelist (and that it should be widespread is significant of the conditions that produced him) has certainly its part in the success with which he has got himself accepted as a mind. The seriousness with which he takes himself as a novelist is complete – if seriousness can be so ineffably blank, so unaware. Explaining why he should have cut short a brilliant career (we are to understand) as a scientist, he tells us that it had always been his vocation to be a writer. And he assumes with a happy and undoubting matter-of-factness – the signs are unmistakable – that his sense of vocation has been triumphantly vindicated and that he is beyond question a novelist of a high order (of 'world-class' even, to adopt his own idiom). Confidence so astonishingly enjoyed might politely be called memorable – if one could imagine the memory of Snow the novelist long persisting; but it won't, it can't, in spite of the British Council's brochure on him (he is a British Council classic).[3] I say 'astonishingly enjoyed', for as a novelist he doesn't exist; he doesn't begin to exist. He can't be said to know what a novel is. The nonenity is apparent on every page of his fictions – consistently manifested, whatever aspect of a novel one looks for. I am trying to remember where I heard (can I have dreamed it?) that they are composed for him by an electronic brain called Charlie, into which the instructions are fed in the form of the chapter-headings. However that may be, he – or the brain (if that's the explanation) – can't do any of the things the power to do which makes a novelist. He tells you what you are to take him as doing, but he can give you no more than the telling. When the characters are supposed to fall in love you are told they do, but he can't show it happening. Abundant dialogue assures you that this is the novelistic art, but never was dialogue more inept; to imagine it spoken is impossible. And Snow is helpless to suggest character in speech. He announces in his chapter-headings the themes and developments in which we are to see the significance of what follows, but what follows adds nothing to the effect of the announcement, and there is no more significance in the completed book than there is drama – or life. It is not merely that Snow can't make his characters live for us – that he lacks *that* creative power; the characters as he thinks of them are so impoverished in the interests they are supposed to have and to represent that even if they had been made to live, one would have asked of them, individually and in the lump: 'What of life is there here, and what significance capable of engaging an educated mind *could* be conveyed through such representatives of humanity?'

Among the most current novels of Snow's are those which offer to depict from the inside the senior academic world of Cambridge, and they suggest as characteristic of that world lives and dominant interests of such unrelieved and cultureless banality that, if one could credit Snow's art with any power of imaginative impact, one would say that he had done his university much harm – for this is a time when the image of the ancient university that is entertained at large matters immensely.[4] Even when he makes a suspect piece of research central to his plot, as in that feeble exercise, *The Affair*, he does no more than a very incompetent manufacturer of whodunnits could do: no corresponding intellectual interest comes into the novel; science is a mere word, the vocation merely postulated.[5] It didn't take a brilliant research scientist to deal with the alleged piece of research as Snow deals with it – or a scientist of any kind. Both George Eliot and Lawrence could have made such a theme incomparably more real.

What the novelist really believes in, the experience he identifies his profoundest ego with because it makes him feel himself a distinguished man and a lord of life, is given us in Lewis Eliot. Eliot has inhabited the Corridors of Power; that is what really matters; that is what qualifies him to look down upon these dons, the scientists as well as the literary intellectuals, with a genially 'placing' wisdom from above; there we have the actual Snow, who, I repeat, is a portent of our civilization; there we have the explanation of his confident sense of importance, which, in an extraordinary way, becomes where his writing is concerned a conviction of genius: he has known from inside the Corridors of Power.[6] That he has really *been* a scientist, that science as such has ever, in any important inward way, existed for him, there is no evidence in his fiction.

And I have to say now that in *The Two Cultures and the Scientific Revolution* there is no evidence, either. The only presence science has is as a matter of external reference, entailed in a show of knowledgeableness. Of qualities that one might set to the credit of a scientific training there are none. As far as the internal evidence goes, the lecture was conceived and written by someone who had not had the advantage of an intellectual discipline of any kind. I was on the point of illustrating this truth from Snow's way with the term 'culture' – a term so important for his purposes. By way of enforcing his testimony that the scientists 'have their own culture', he tells us: 'This culture contains a great deal of argument, usually much more rigorous, and almost always at a higher conceptual level, than literary persons' arguments.' But the argument of Snow's Rede lecture is at an immensely *lower* conceptual level, and incomparably more loose and inconsequent, than any I myself, a literary person, should permit in a group discussion I was conducting, let alone a pupil's essay.

Thought, it is true, in the field in which Snow challenges us, doesn't admit of control by strict definition of the key terms; but the more fully one realizes this the more aware will one be of the need to cultivate a vigilant responsibility in using them, and an alert consciousness of any changes of force they may incur as the argument passes from context to context. And what I have to say is that Snow's argument proceeds with so extreme a *naïveté* of unconsciousness and irresponsibility that to call it a movement of thought is to flatter it.

Take the confident ease of his way with what he calls 'the Literary Culture', that one of his opposed pair which, as a novelist, he feels himself qualified to present to us with a peculiar personal authority. He identifies 'the Literary Culture' with, to use his own phrase, the 'literary intellectual' – by which he means the modish literary world; his 'intellectual' is the intellectual of the *New Statesman* circle and the reviewing in the Sunday papers. Snow accepts this 'culture' implicitly as the *haute culture* of our time; he takes it as representing the age's finer consciousness so far as a culture ignorant of science can. He, we are to understand, has it, and at the same time the scientific culture; he unites the two. I can't help remarking that this suggested equivalence (equivalence at any rate in reality) must constitute for me, a literary person, the gravest suspicion regarding the scientific one of Snow's two cultures. For his 'literary culture' is something that those genuinely interested in literature can only regard with contempt and resolute hostility. Snow's 'literary intellectual' is the enemy of art and life.

Note with what sublime, comic and frightening ease (for this sage is after all a Cambridge man) Snow, without any sense of there having been a shift, slips from his 'literary culture' into 'the traditional culture'. The feat of innocent unawareness is striking and significant enough when he is talking of the contemporary scene. But when, with the same ease, he carries the matter-of-fact identification into the past – 'the traditional culture', he tells us, with reference to the Industrial Revolution, 'didn't notice: or when it did notice, didn't like what it saw' – the significance becomes so portentous as to be hardly credible. But Snow, we must remind ourselves, *is* frightening in his capacity of representative phenomenon. He knows nothing of history. He pronounces about it with as complete a confidence as he pronounces about literature (French, Russian and American as well as English), but he is equally ignorant of both. He has no notion of the changes in civilization that have produced his 'literary culture' and made it possible for C. P. Snow to enjoy a status of distinguished intellectual, have the encouragement of knowing that his Rede lecture is earnestly studied in sixth forms, and be (with practical consequences) an authority in the field of higher education: things that the real, the living, 'traditional culture' (for there is a reality answering to that phrase) can no more countenance today than it could have foreseen them in the nineteenth century.

The intellectual nullity apparent in his way with the term 'culture' is only emphasized for us when, coming to his other culture, that of the scientist, he makes, as himself a scientist, his odd show of a concern for a 'high conceptual level'. 'At one pole,' he says, 'the scientific culture really is a culture, not only in an intellectual, but also in an anthropological sense.' The offered justification for that 'anthropological sense' is given, we find, if we examine the context, in this sentence: 'Without thinking about it they respond alike.' Snow adds: 'That is what a culture means.' We needn't bother one way or the other about the 'anthropological'; what is certain is that Snow gives us here a hint worth taking up. He, of course, is supposed to be thinking, and thinking profoundly, in that Rede lecture, but actually it is a perfect document of the kind of 'culture', to use his word, that he here defines – defines, even though unconscious of the full significance of what he says, the formal definition getting its completion and charge from the whole context – that is, from the actual performance. His unconsciousness is an essential characteristic. 'Without thinking, they respond alike': Snow's habits as an intellectual and a sage were formed in such a milieu. Thinking is a difficult art and requires training and practice in any given field. It is a pathetic and comic – and menacing – illusion on Snow's part that he is capable of thought on the problems he offers to advise us on. If his lecture has any value for use in schools – or universities – it is as a document for the study of cliché.

We think of cliché commonly as a matter of style. But style is a habit of expression, and a habit of expression that runs to the cliché tells us something adverse about the quality of the thought expressed. 'History is merciless to failure': Snow makes play with a good many propositions of that kind – if 'proposition' is the right word. We call them clichés because, though Snow clearly feels that he is expressing thought, the thought, considered even for a moment, is seen to be a mere phantom, and Snow's illusion is due to the fact that he is *not* thinking, but resting inertly (though with a sense of power) on vague memories of the way in which he had heard (or seen) such phrases used. They carry for him – he belonging to what he calls a 'culture' – a charge of currency-value which is independent of first-hand, that is, actual, thinking. He would be surprised if he were told they are clichés.

He would be still more surprised to be told it is cliché when, describing the distinctive traits of his scientists, he says: 'they have the future in their bones'. He clearly feels that it has an idiosyncratic speech-raciness that gives his wisdom a genial authority. But it is basic cliché – for Snow's pretensions, more damagingly cliché than the kind of thing I instanced first, for it dismisses the issue, tacitly eliminates the problem, discussion of which would have been the *raison d'être* of the lecture if Snow had been capable of the preoccupation, and the accordant exercise of thought, he advertises.

Such a phrase as 'they have the future in their bones' (and Snow repeats it) cannot be explained as a meaningful proposition, and in that sense has no meaning. It emerges spontaneously from the cultural world to which Snow belongs and it registers uncritically (hence the self-evident force it has for him) its assumptions and attitudes and ignorances. That world, I was on the point of saying, is the world of his 'scientific culture', but I might equally have said that it is the world of the *New Statesman*, the *Guardian* and the Sunday papers. And Snow rides on an advancing swell of cliché: this exhilarating motion is what he takes for inspired and authoritative thought.

He brings out the intended commendatory force, and the actual large significance, of 'they have the future in their bones' (there is nothing else by way of clarification) by telling us antithetically of the representatives of 'the traditional culture': 'they are natural Luddites'. It is a *general* charge, and he makes quite plain that he includes in it the creators of English literature in the nineteenth century and the twentieth. The upshot is that if you insist on the need for any other kind of concern, entailing forethought, action and provision, about the human future – any other kind of misgiving – than that which talks in terms of productivity, material standards of living, hygienic and technological progress, then you are a Luddite. Snow's position, for all the mess of clichés and sentimental banalities that constitutes his style, is unequivocal.

It might seem an odd position for one who proudly thinks of himself as a major novelist. But I now come to the point when I have again to say, with a more sharply focused intention this time, that Snow not only hasn't in him the beginnings of a novelist; he is utterly without a glimmer of what creative literature is, or why it matters. That significant truth comes home to us, amusingly but finally, when, near his opening, he makes a point of impressing on us that, as himself a creative writer, he is humanly (shall I say)? supremely well qualified – that he emphatically *has* a soul. 'The individual condition of each of us,' he tells us, 'is tragic,' and, by way of explaining that statement, he adds, 'we die alone'. Once he says 'we live alone', but in general – for he makes his point redundantly – he prefers to stress dying; it's more solemn. He is enforcing a superiority to be recognized in the scientists: they, he says, 'see no reason why, just because the individual condition is tragic, so must the social condition be'. For himself, with tragic stoicism, he says, 'we die alone: all right,' but – which is his message, the sum of his wisdom – 'there is social hope'.

He is repetitious, but he develops no explanation further than this. It doesn't occur to him that there is any need, stultifying as anyone capable of thought can see the antithesis to be. What *is* the 'social condition' that has nothing to do with the 'individual condition'? What is the 'social hope' that transcends, cancels or makes indifferent the inescapable tragic condition of each individual? Where, if not in individuals, is what is hoped for – a *non*-tragic condition, one supposes – to be located? Or are we to find the reality of life in hoping for other people a kind of felicity about which as proposed for ourselves ('jam', Snow calls it later – we die alone, but there's jam to be had first) we have no illusions? Snow's pompous phrases give us the central and supreme instance of what I have called 'basic cliché'. He takes over inertly – takes over as a self-evident simple clarity – the characteristic and disastrous confusion of the civilization he is offering to instruct.

It is a confusion to which all creative writers are tacit enemies. The greatest English writer of our century dealt with it explicitly – dealt with it again and again, in many ways, and left to our hand what should be the classical exposure. But Snow, exhibiting his inwardness with modern literature by enumerating the writers who above all matter, leaves Lawrence out (though he offers us Wyndham Lewis – the brutal and boring Wyndham Lewis). Lawrence, intent with all his being on the nature and movement of the civilization of the West, turned the intelligence of genius on what I have called the characteristic confusion. He diagnoses it in his supreme novel, *Women in Love*, both discursively and by the poetic means of a great novelist. Concerned with enforcing in relation to what may be called a quintessential presentment of the modern world the Laurentian maxim that 'nothing matters but life', he insists on the truth that only in living individuals is life there, and individual lives cannot be aggregated or equated or dealt with quantitatively in any way.

The provocation for the insistence in the place I have in mind is given by the word 'equality', and the context in which the word is introduced may be suggested by saying that the liberal-idealist sage and social philosopher, Sir Joshua Mattheson, who figures in *Women in Love* reminds us irresistibly of Bertrand Russell (something of a paradigmatic hero for Snow, who is himself the spiritual son of H. G. Wells). The Lawrence-like Birkin of Lawrence's novel says: 'I want every man to have his share in the world's goods, so that I am rid of his importunity....' The un-Lawrentian tone given by 'rid' and 'importunity' belongs to the dramatic Birkin and the dramatic context, but in what Birkin has just said we have pure Lawrence: '"We are all different and unequal in spirit – it is only the social differences that are based on accidental material conditions. We are all abstractly and mathematically equal, if you like. Every man has hunger and thirst, two eyes, one nose and two legs. We're all the same in point of number. But spiritually, there is pure difference and neither equality nor inequality counts."'[7]

The point is intimately related to that which Lawrence makes when he says that few people live on the spot where they are – which is equivalent to saying that few people really live. Snow, in exhorting us to put aside our individual living and live instead on 'social hope', preaches as the way of salvation the characteristic modern mode of refusing to live on the spot where one is. 'Live', of course, is a word of many possible values, as great novelists and poets make us know. Snow, refraining from permitting himself a morbid consciousness of his individual tragedy, enjoys a personal life, I suspect, that gives him considerable satisfaction – being a sage, a familiar of the Corridors of Power, a member of the Athenæum, a great figure in the Sunday papers, a great novelist, a maker of young novelists, a maker (perhaps) of academic careers. He can hardly, for the myriads for whom he generously entertains 'social hope', plan or foresee lives that will be filled with satisfaction and significance in that way. But what primarily calls for emphasis is the poverty of Snow's ostensible range of satisfactions – which is a poverty of his own canons, and of his sense of significance; a poverty in considering which one finds oneself considering the inadequacy of his sense of human nature and human need.

The significance of his blankness in the face of literature is immense. It is a significance the more damning (in relation to his pretensions) because of the conviction with which he offers himself as an authority on the literature of the present and the past. I didn't exaggerate when I said that he doesn't know what literature is. Every pronouncement he makes about it – and he makes a great many – enforces that truth. Illustrating his notion of the important kind of relation between art and life, the writer and the contemporary world, he tells us that the Russians (he knows all about Russian literature) 'are as ready to cope in art with the processes of production as Balzac was with the processes of craft manufacture'. But, for those preoccupied with the problems Snow confronts us with, unintentionally, literature has its immediate and crucial relevance because of the kind of writer who asks, who lives in his art and makes *us* live, kinds of question that, except as conventional profundities to which one should sometimes lift one's hat, seem never to have come within Snow's cognizance (an effect only emphasized by his 'tragic' and 'we die alone' – which belong, of course, to the most abject journalism). What for – what ultimately for? What, ultimately, do men live by? These questions are in and of the creative drive that produces great art in Conrad and Lawrence (to instance two very different novelists of the century who haven't, one gathers, impressed Snow).

Take, as a simple illustration, Conrad's *The Shadow Line*, and note – well, note everything, but note particularly the evocation of the young master's inner response when he first sets eyes on his ship, his first command.[8] The urgent creative exploring represented by the questions is immeasurably more complex in *Women in Love*, a comprehensive and intensely 'engaged' study of modern civilization. Of course, to such questions there can't be, in any ordinary sense of the word, 'answers', and the effect as of total 'answer' differs as between Conrad and Lawrence, or as between any two great writers. But life in the civilization of an age for which such creative questioning is not done and is not influential on general sensibility tends characteristically to lack a dimension: it tends to have no depth – no depth against which it doesn't tacitly protect itself by the habit of unawareness (so Snow enjoins us to do our living in the dimension of 'social hope'). In coming to terms with great literature we discover what at bottom we really believe. What for – what ultimately for? What do men live by? – the questions work and tell at what I can only call a religious depth of thought and feeling. Perhaps, with my eye on the adjective, I may just recall for you Tom Brangwen, in *The Rainbow*, watching by the fold in lambing-time under the night-sky: 'He knew he did not belong to himself.'[9]

It is characteristic of Snow that 'believe' for him should be a very simple word. 'Statistically,' he says, 'I suppose slightly more scientists are in religious terms unbelievers, compared with the rest of the intellectual world.' There are believers and unbelievers; we all know what 'religious terms' are; and everything relevant in relation to the adjective has been said. Snow goes on at once: 'Statistically, I suppose slightly more scientists are on the Left in open politics.' The *naïveté* is complete; it is a *naïveté* indistinguishable from the portentous ignorance. The ignorance is that which appears as historical ignorance in his account of the Industrial Revolution, and its consequences, in the nineteenth century. It manifests itself as a terrifying confidence of simplification – terrifying because of the distortions and falsifications it entails, and the part it plays in that spirit of practical wisdom about the human future of which Snow's Rede lecture might be called a classic. Disposing with noble scorn of a wholly imaginary kind of opposition to his crass Wellsianism, he says (and *this* is his history – and his logic): 'For, with singular unanimity, in any country where they have had the chance, the poor have walked off the land into the factories as fast as the factories could take them.' This, of course, is mere brute assertion, callous in its irresponsibility. But it is essential to Snow's wisdom. If one points out that the actual history has been, with significance for one's apprehension of the full human problem, incomparably and poignantly more complex than that, Snow dismisses one as a 'natural Luddite'. He dismisses so – sees no further significance in – Dickens and Ruskin, and all the writers leading down to Lawrence. Yet – to confine myself to the non-creative writer, about whom the challenged comment is most easily made – it was Ruskin who put into currency the distinction between wealth and well-being, which runs down through Morris and the British Socialist movement to the Welfare State.[10]

But for Ruskin 'well-being' or 'welfare' could not conceivably be matters of merely material standard of living, with the advantages of technology and scientific hygiene. And there we have the gap – the gap that is the emptiness beneath Snow's ignorance – between Snow and not only Ruskin, but the great creative writers of the century before Snow: they don't exist for him; nor does civilization. Pressing on this ancient university his sense of the urgency of the effort to which we must give ourselves, he says: 'Yet' – in spite, that is, of the 'horror' which, he says, is 'hard to look at straight' – 'yet they've proved that common men can show astonishing fortitude in chasing jam tomorrow. Jam today, and men aren't at their most exciting: jam tomorrow, and one often sees them at their noblest. The transformations have also provided something which only the scientific culture can take in its stride.

70

Yet, when we don't take it in our stride, it makes us look silly.'

The callously ugly insensitiveness of the mode of expression is wholly significant. It gives us Snow, who is wholly representative of the world, or culture, to which it belongs. It is the world in which Mr Macmillan said – or might, taking a tip from Snow, have varied his phrase by saying – 'You never had so much jam'; and in which, if you are enlightened, you see that the sum of wisdom lies in expediting the processes which will ensure the Congolese, the Indonesians, the Bushmen (no, not the Bushmen – there aren't enough of them), the Chinese, the Indians, *their* increasing supplies of jam.[11] It is the world in which the vital inspiration, the creative drive, is 'Jam tomorrow' (if you haven't any today) or (if you have it today) '*More* jam tomorrow'. It is the world in which, even at the level of the intellectual weeklies, 'standard of living' is an ultimate criterion, its raising an ultimate aim, a matter of wages and salaries and what you can buy with them, reduced hours of work, and the technological resources that make your increasing leisure worth having, so that productivity – the supremely important thing – must be kept on the rise, at whatever cost to protesting conservative habit.

Don't mistake me. I am not preaching that we should defy, or try to reverse, the accelerating movement of external civilization (the phrase sufficiently explains itself, I hope) that is determined by advancing technology. Nor am I suggesting that Snow, in so far as he is advocating improvements in scientific education, is wrong (I suspect he isn't very original). What I *am* saying is that such a concern is not enough – disastrously not enough. Snow himself is proof of that, product as he is of the initial cultural consequences of the kind of rapid change he wants to see accelerated to the utmost and assimilating all the world, bringing (he is convinced), provided we are fore-sighted enough to perceive that no one now will long consent to be without abundant jam, salvation and lasting felicity to all mankind.

It must be recognized, though, that he doesn't *say* 'salvation' or 'felicity', but 'jam'. And if 'jam' means (as it does) the prosperity and leisure enjoyed by our well-to-do working class, then the significant fact not noticed by Snow is that the felicity it represents cannot be regarded by a fully human mind as a matter for happy contemplation. Nor is it felt by the beneficiaries to be satisfying. I haven't time to enlarge on this last point. I will only remark that the observation is not confined to 'natural Luddites': I recently read in the *Economist* a disturbed review of a book by a French sociologist of which the theme is (not a new idea to us) the incapacity of the industrial worker, who – inevitably – looks on real living as reserved for his leisure, to use his leisure in any but essentially passive ways.[12] And this, for me, evokes that total vision which makes Snow's 'social hope' unintoxicating to many of us – the vision of our imminent tomorrow in today's America: the energy, the triumphant technology, the productivity, the high standard of living and the life-impoverishment – the human emptiness; emptiness and boredom craving alcohol – of one kind or another. Who will assert that the average member of a modern society is more fully human, or more alive, than a Bushman, an Indian peasant, or a member of one of those poignantly surviving primitive peoples, with their marvellous art and skills and vital intelligence?

But I will come to the explicit positive note that has all along been my goal (for I am not a Luddite) in this way: the advance of science and technology means a human future of change so rapid and of such kinds, of tests and challenges so unprecedented, of decisions and possible non-decisions so momentous and insidious in their consequences, that mankind – this is surely clear – will need to be in full intelligent possession of its full humanity (and 'possession' here means, not confident ownership of that which belongs to *us* – our property, but a basic living deference towards that to which, opening as it does into the unknown and itself unmeasurable, we know we belong). I haven't chosen to say that mankind will need all its traditional wisdom; that might suggest a kind of conservatism that, so far as I am concerned, is the enemy. What we need, and shall continue to need not less, is something with the livingness of the deepest vital instinct; as intelligence, a power – rooted, strong in experience, and supremely human – of creative response to the new challenges of time; something that is alien to either of Snow's cultures.

His blankness comes out when, intimating (he supposes) that his concern for university reform envisages the total educational function, he tells us how shocking it is that educated people should not be able to appreciate the Shakespeare of science. It simply hasn't occurred to him that to call the master scientific mind (say Rutherford) a Shakespeare is nothing but a cheap journalistic infelicity. He enforces his intention by telling us, after reporting the failure of his literary friends to describe the second law of thermodynamics: 'yet I was asking something which is about the equivalent of *Have you read a work of Shakespeare's?*' There *is* no scientific equivalent of that question;

equations between orders so disparate are meaningless – which is not to say that the Neo-Wellsian assurance that proposes them hasn't *its* significance. More largely, Snow exclaims: 'As though the scientific edifice of the physical world were not, in its intellectual depth, complexity and articulation, the most beautiful and wonderful collective work of the mind of man.'

It is pleasant to think of Snow contemplating, daily perhaps, the intellectual depth, complexity and articulation in all their beauty. But there is a prior human achievement of collaborative creation, a more basic work of the mind of man (and more than the mind), one without which the triumphant erection of the scientific edifice would not have been possible: that is, the creation of the human world, including language. It is one we cannot rest on as something done in the past. It lives in the living creative response to change in the present. I mentioned language because it is in terms of literature that I can most easily make my meaning plain, and because of the answer that seems to me called for by Snow's designs on the university. It is in the study of literature, the literature of one's own language in the first place, that one comes to recognize the nature and priority of the third realm (as, unphilosophically, no doubt, I call it, talking with my pupils), the realm of that which is neither merely private and personal nor public in the sense that it can be brought into the laboratory or pointed to. You cannot point to the poem; it is 'there' only in the re-creative response of individual minds to the black marks on the page. But – a necessary faith – it is something in which minds can meet. The process in which this faith is justified is given fairly enough in an account of the nature of criticism.[13] A judgment is personal or it is nothing; you cannot take over someone else's. The implicit form of a judgment is: This is so, isn't it? The question is an appeal for confirmation that the thing *is* so; implicitly that, though expecting, characteristically, an answer in the form, 'yes, but – ' the 'but' standing for qualifications, reserves, corrections. Here we have a diagram of the collaborative-creative process in which the poem comes to be established as something 'out there', of common access in what is in some sense a public world. It gives us, too, the nature of the existence of English literature, a living whole that can have its life only in the living present, in the creative response of individuals, who collaboratively renew and perpetuate what they participate in – a cultural community or consciousness. More, it gives us the nature in general of what I have called the 'third realm' to which all that makes us human belongs.[14]

Perhaps I need say no more by way of enforcing my conviction that, for the sake of our humanity – our humanness, for the sake of a human future, we must do, with intelligent resolution and with faith, all we can to maintain the full life in the present – and life is growth – of our transmitted culture. Like Snow I look to the university. Unlike Snow, I am concerned to make it really a university, something (that is) more than a collocation of specialist departments – to make it a centre of human consciousness: perception, knowledge, judgment and responsibility. And perhaps I have sufficiently indicated on what lines I would justify my seeing the centre of a university in a vital English School.[15] I mustn't say more now about what I mean by that, I will only say that the academic is the enemy and that the academic *can* be beaten, as we who ran *Scrutiny* for twenty years proved.[16] We were, and knew we were, Cambridge – the essential Cambridge in spite of Cambridge: that gives you the spirit of what I have in mind. Snow gets on with what he calls 'the traditional culture' better than I do. To impress us with his anti-academic astringency, he tells us of the old Master of Jesus who said about trains running into Cambridge on Sunday: 'It is equally displeasing to God and to myself.' More to the point is that *that*, I remember, was very much the attitude of the academic powers when, thirty years ago, I wrote a pioneering book on modern poetry that made Eliot a key figure and proposed a new chart, and again when I backed Lawrence as a great writer.[17]

It is assumed, I believe, that work in the scientific departments must be in close touch with the experimental-creative front. In the same way, for the university English School there is a creative front with which, of its function and nature, the School must be in the closest relation. I am not thinking of the fashionable idea that the right qualification for a teaching post is to be a poet – or a commercially successful novelist. I am thinking again of what *Scrutiny* stood – and stands – for: of the creative work it did on the contemporary intellectual-cultural frontier in maintaining the critical function. I must not try now to say more about the way in which such a school would generate in the university a centre of consciousness (and conscience) for our civilization. I will merely insist that it is not inconceivable that Cambridge might become a place where the culture of the Sunday papers was not taken to represent the best that is thought and known in our time.

If so, it is conceivable, perhaps, that the journalistic addiction of our academic intellectuals – and journalism (in one form or another) is now the menacing disease of university 'English' – might, at Cambridge, be pretty generally recognized for the thing it is. In such a Cambridge the attention I have paid to a Snow would be unnecessary.

Prefatory note to the Chatto edition (1962)

The abundant adverse comment directed against my lecture hasn't advanced the argument by leaving me something to answer. The *Spectator* was indulgent when it called the mass of correspondence it printed a 'debate'. I say 'adverse comment' because to say 'criticism' would be inappropriate: the case I presented wasn't dealt with – there was no attempt to deal with it. The angry, abusive and strikingly confident utterances of Snow's supporters merely illustrated the nature of the world or 'culture' that had made Snow a mind, a sage, and a major novelist. 'Without thinking they respond alike.' The confidence is remarkable and significant because the demonstrators see themselves, unmistakably, as an intellectual *élite* and preeminently capable of grounded conviction, and yet, when they sense criticism by which their distinction and standing are implicitly denied, can only, with the flank-rubber's response, enact an involuntary corroboration of the criticism.

The lecture and its reception go on being referred to a great deal: there is reason, I think, for making generally accessible in print what I actually said. The issues are alive and momentous, and Sir Charles Snow's *The Two Cultures* seems likely to go on circulating – in schools and

77

elsewhere. I have to thank Mr Yudkin for letting me print his article along with my lecture.[†] It didn't come to my notice till the lecture had been delivered and had appeared in the *Spectator*. And Mr Yudkin's criticism was wholly independent of mine: it had been published (in the *Cambridge Review*) a good while before my Richmond lecture had been thought of.

It might in a sense have been said to make my lecture unnecessary. But it puts what seems to me the unanswerable case against Snow from another approach than mine: Mr Yudkin is a research scientist (biochemist). And such a concurrence (for it is essentially that) arrived at from approaches so different seems to me to give decided point to the printing of the two critical formulations together. In my lecture, of course, my criticism of *The Two Cultures* subserves a preoccupation with a positive theme and advocacy of my own. But my argument *is*, very largely, the criticism, which is inseparable from the presentment of the positive theme. I know too, from many letters I have received from both sides of the Atlantic, that Snow, though widely thought of as 'public relations man' for Science, is far from being regarded with favour by all scientists. Nor had I supposed, or meant to imply, otherwise. In any case, I feel it impossible to believe that scientists in considerable numbers will not acclaim Mr Yudkin's criticism of Snow as sound – and salutary.

I have said enough by way of explaining the decision to print the two independently conceived critiques in association.

[†] It is to be found together with *Two Cultures? – The Significance of C. P. Snow* as published separately (Chatto & Windus).

Prefatory note to the US edition (1963)

My lecture was given in England. The above paragraphs, written as a 'Prefatory Note', were addressed to a British public. I knew, however, that Snow had received much publicity in America, and that Professor Lionel Trilling, in the New York review *Commentary* (June 1962), had thought it worth while criticizing my lecture for a public that, for the most part, couldn't have read it.[18] And when, in the above 'Note', I made my dismissing comment on my critics I wasn't intending to except Trilling: it seemed to me that he too had made no attempt to deal as a disinterested critic with what I had actually said. That is, no rejoinder was called for; he had my answer there already before him in my lecture. A general charge he brings against me is the one thing I think worth adverting to in particular here. I will say a little about it because I can at the same time indicate all there is any point in saying about another critic of my lecture whom I know to have addressed an American audience: Professor Richard Wollheim in *Partisan Review* (spring 1962).[19]

'There can be no two opinions,' says Professor Trilling, 'about the tone in which Dr Leavis deals with Sir Charles.' More particularly the charge is that my references to Snow's novels were gratuitous, not being necessary to my theme and argument. They are cruel in their gratuitousness, we are to gather: they are expressed, characteristically (Professor Trilling intimates), in a way calculated to cause unnecessary pain and offence. I have to comment that, in thus lending himself to the general cry that I have 'attacked' Snow (and 'attack' goes with the suggestion that

I have indulged in an unpleasant display of personal animus), Professor Trilling, who passes as a vindicator of the critical function, seems to me guilty of *la trahison des clercs*. His attitude would make the essential work of the critic today impossible. It belongs to the ethos I was intent on challenging.

In my lecture I deal with certain menacing characteristics of our civilization. Snow, I start by emphasizing, is a *portent*; a portent in that, while he is in himself without distinction of any kind, so that it is ridiculous to credit him with any capacity for serious thinking about the problems on which he offers to advise the world, he has been accepted very widely in England (and in America too, I believe) as a powerful and diversely gifted mind and an authoritative voice of wisdom. If one calls attention to the clear truth about such a portent in a way that exposes to the full light of publicity the unanswerableness of the constatation, then, of course, the critical or hygienic process that achieved the result aimed at may fairly be called (what it necessarily had to be) drastic, and the portent as person may very well feel 'wounded', leaving his friends to accuse one of 'cruelty'. But those critics who call me, the perpetrator of the Richmond lecture, cruel – what excuse have they? None, I think. But the significance is clear: they have played their part in the creating of the portent, they have underwritten – at least tacitly – the Intellect and the Sage, and they cry out with so intense an animus against the damaging constatation because its truth is so unanswerably clear. The unanswerableness is the 'cruelty' and is what has 'wounded' Snow. It would have been less 'cruel' if it had been accompanied, as it was not, by the animus that impels the intention to hurt.[‡]

My lecture has no personal animus in it: the kind of drastic finality I aimed at in my dismissal of the Intellect and Sage was incompatible with that. But, of course, if by a sharpness, clarity and cogency of challenge that make it hardly possible not to see the 'cruel' truth you undo the publicity-work that has made a great public figure out of a person of undistinguished capacities, that person must inevitably feel that he has suffered an odious experience – one that he will identify with an unfeeling and destructive 'attack'. For anyone, however, who has made a name as concerned for a high intellectual standard and critical integrity to join with the 'victim's' friends and allies in passing on the public that kind of identification as a just criticism of the critic is (as I have said) no better than *trahison des clercs*.

For the supersession, in what should be the field of real intellectual and spiritual authority, of serious criteria by the power of creating publicity-values is a frightening manifestation of the way our civilization is going. It is a concomitant of the technological revolution. The kind of standards that concern the literary critic (say) can be 'there' for him to appeal to only in the existence of a public that can respond intelligently to the challenge and make its response felt. I have no doubt that there are in England today (I confine myself to speaking of my own

---

[‡] I was not warned of the editor's intention to insert cartoons into the text of my lecture as printed in the *Spectator*, and he had my indignant protest.

country) the elements of such a public; there are a great many cultivated and responsible individuals, and they may be regarded as forming some sort of intellectual community. But it is not in anything like a full sense a community; the consequences of the technological revolution preclude its being a public in the way the critic needs.

Organs addressing the 'educated' public require in our time large circulations in order to satisfy the advertisement manager and subsist. The so-called 'quality' Sunday papers (the *Observer* and the *Sunday Times*), for instance, must attract and hold their million readers, and they can hope to do so only by catering at a level of appeal realistically calculated in relation to a mass public of the kind (that of the class-consciously superior middle classes, business and professional). They make a show, that is, of observing the standards of taste, education and serious intellectual interest of *haute culture*, while actually supplying 'magazine' diversion and gossip-fodder for the relaxed middlebrow. They maintain in their review pages – an aspect of this cultural phenomenon that, with my eye on my theme, I have to emphasize – the air and the reputation of performing the critical function at the highest level, their reviewers being (it is to be understood) of the intellectual élite. And indeed they are, if anything properly to be called an intellectual élite anywhere presents itself in British journalism. The critical function is performed at no higher level in the intellectual weeklies, where in fact we find not only the same kind of writer, but very largely the same names.

And here I come to an observation that must be seen, I suppose, as pointing to a marked difference between what an American with my interests and anxieties would report and what one has to reckon with in the aspect of British civilization I myself am contemplating. For America is not a tight little island, and Great Britain is. How little and how tight is brought home to one when, thinking that the preposterous and menacing absurdity of a C. P. Snow's consecrated public standing shouldn't remain longer undealt with, one challenges recognition for the patent fact that the Emperor is naked. One finds arrayed against one a comprehensive system of personal relations, the members of which (even though the use of the Christian name may not mean much)§ know they 'belong', and observe a corresponding code.[20]

The system has its literary-journalistic organs and foci and its institutional centres, and at the midmost, wholly in its possession on the literary side, is the BBC, with its organ *The Listener*. The BBC is an immensely potent means of giving general currency to the values of the metropolitan literary world – that which Snow calls 'the traditional culture', meaning the *élite* he supposes himself to mingle with in the *New Statesman* circle – and of getting them accepted as the 'best that is thought and known in our time'. These values can be the merest publicity-creations, created by iteration, symphonic suggestion, and the authority of the 'intellectuals' of the system, as Snow the Sage and distinguished novelist was.

Not that I suppose there weren't a number of his literary-intellectual friends who preferred not to seek opportunities to express publicly a conviction of his

---

§ It is a significant index. Thus Dame Edith Sitwell pronounced for publication, 'Dr Leavis only attacked Charles because he is famous and writes good English.'

creative genius. For his incapacity as a novelist plainly is what, in my lecture, I say it is – total. He seems to me almost unreadable. Yet a great number of copies of his novels is to be found in every public library, and they go out a great deal. The explanation can be seen in the fact that Snow has been a major subject for lecture-directed study in WEA classes[**] and in adult education generally. And it is not only Snow's Rede lecture that is pushed for devout study on the young (our future educated class) in the upper forms of grammar schools; his novels are too. Are they not contemporary classics? And does not the British Council endorse that estimate? – the British Council, that characteristic British institution which, financed out of public funds and well-regarded by the Foreign Office, fosters the repute of British culture abroad (though not, I believe, in the United States), and, for the instruction of the world, issues on British writers (picked by itself) brochures that sell immensely at home and are to be found in every Cambridge bookshop.

A scrutiny of this British Council literature of guidance and currency-promotion will reveal that the ethos, the sense of values, the critical enlightenment it serves are those of what I have called the metropolitan literary world – the cultural world of Sir Charles Snow's 'literary intellectual'. The British Council, in fact, is another institutional centre for that world, and, like the BBC, is taken full advantage of as such. How much that is other than robust good conscience there may be in all this it is, in the nature of things, such a state of affairs having

[**] Workers' Educational Association, a democratic organization for adult education.

become established, difficult to say; in fact, the question hardly applies. But the system is quick to react to the threat represented by any criticism that seems to challenge its ethos; by any implicit reminder, that is, of serious standards. Such reminders cannot be tolerated; it is a matter of self-preservation. The resources of the system are deployed against the offending critic or 'influence'; if he can't be suppressed he must be, by any means, discredited. For the 'literary world' has to maintain its sense, and the general illusion, of its own comprehensiveness. It is immune from control by the educated public – the intellectual and spiritual community in which, so far as in this technological civilization it can be effectively appealed to and can make its response felt, standards are 'there' to be evoked by the critic. The 'literary world' is its own public – the only one it, normally, is conscious of. It hates the suggestion that there might be another, one to be feared: a real educated public that doesn't take the 'literary world' seriously.

The 'literary world', in fact, with its command of all the means of publicity, virtually shuts off the educated public from effective existence. This public, in any serious sense of the noun, is only a potential public. It has no part in the formation of contemporary taste, no power to influence or to check – I am thinking of what passes for educated taste.

Though I spoke of the 'literary world' as 'metropolitan', I wasn't forgetting that, most significantly, an essential element in it (and I don't mean my 'literary' to be taken in a narrow sense – I am thinking of what, borrowing a licence from Snow, I will call the whole publicity-created culture) belongs to the universities. I refer to this fact and its significance in the close of my lecture. That Snow should have been chosen as Rede lecturer at Cambridge, that his lecture should have passed there as a distinguished intellectual performance, and that his novels should be supposed by Classical dons to be contemporary literature – these things can't be seen as surprising: they are representative. It wouldn't be at all ridiculous to conjecture that Snow might have decisive influence in academic appointments – and on the side of the humanities.[21]

Here, then, we have the cultural consequences of the technological revolution. And to Professor Wollheim, who charges me (so far as I can understand him) with insidious and significant evasion in not saying clearly whether I am for a high material standard of living or against it, I reply that the problem I am concerned with cannot be reduced to those terms, and that in insisting that it can he ignores the whole theme, argument and substance of my lecture, and that, if he really reads it, he will find my answer to the given charge in the place where I deal with Snow's use of 'Luddite' – and elsewhere. What I have contended, giving my reasons as forcibly as in an hour's discourse I could, is that we mustn't regard these cultural consequences as inevitable, or acquiesce in their being accepted mechanically and unconsciously, and that a preoccupation and an effort of a very different kind from any contemplated by Snow are necessary. And I have to add that, in his ability to ignore my theme as he does, Professor Wollheim, who is a philosopher, seems to me himself a portent.

As for Professor Trilling's charge that my bringing Snow's novels into my argument was a gratuitously offensive irrelevance, I find it hard to understand how he can have persuaded himself that he was justified in making it. Is it true that, as I have heard, he has committed himself in print to a favourable opinion of Snow the novelist? If so, does he still hold it?

Professor Wollheim's suggestion ('the sheltered atmosphere of the hall at Downing College') that the Press and the BBC were excluded from my lecture because I wished to be protected against critical reactions is oddly wide of the mark. The Richmond lecture is private, and I, who was merely the person invited to give it in 1962, certainly didn't want it to be made the occasion of the ugly kind of publicity it actually got – and would inevitably get, if the Press were given a chance. And I was intent on ensuring that my actual theme and argument should be really attended to. I should have indeed been a fool if I had thought that giving the journalists an opportunity was likely to further that aim. My purpose was to see to the publication of the full text myself. It will be supposed that, in so far as I had been sanguine, Professor Trilling's and Professor Wollheim's responses to the text as it appeared in the *Spectator* brought me some disillusion.

Luddites?
Or, There is Only One Culture (1966)

~

I am used to being misrepresented, but not resigned to it. Everyone who has committed himself in relation to the themes I discussed in my Richmond lecture, *Two Cultures? – The Significance of C. P. Snow*, and taken a line at all like that taken by me there, knows how gross and inconsequent is the misrepresentation that follows, and how impossible it is to get the case one has put attended to. Instead, something quite different is, explicitly and implicitly, associated with one's name and made the target for a routine play of contemptuous and dismissing reference. Of course, this kind of response represents a large element of willed refusal to see and understand – the will not recognizing itself for the thing it is by reason of a flank-rubbing consensus that is its sanction. But this element of refusal is an essential characteristic of the situation that the persuader has to deal with, and therefore, if one thinks the issues are of moment – and I do, one is not resigned.

You see, I am confessing to a touch of embarrassment: I don't want to seem to be attributing any of that unintelligent – or anti-intelligence – set of the will to the present audience as a general characterizing trait, but, in presenting as clearly as I can in positive terms and in a positive spirit (which is what I want to do) my view of the issues raised by the talk about the 'two cultures', I am bound to refer to the misrepresentations and misunderstandings that ought not by now to need answering but seem all the same to be the staple enlightenment about these issues so far as the publicity-practitioners, the formers of public opinion, are concerned.

And that, I must emphasize, is not merely at the lowest level. Richard Wollheim, for example, who is a Professor of Philosophy, remarked in *Partisan Review*, with an air of convicting me of insidious and significant evasion, that I had not in my Richmond lecture made clear whether I was *for* a high material standard of living or *against* it. My point of course had been this: that it won't do to make a rising material standard of living the self-sufficient aim on the confident assumption that we needn't admit any other kind of consideration, any more adequate recognition of human nature and human need, into the incitement and direction of our thinking and our effort: technological and material advance and fair distribution – it's enough, it's the only true responsibility, to concentrate on them; that's the attitude I confront.

Again, to take a very representative example of the habit of those who address the British intelligentsia, a writer in the *Spectator*, Sarah Gainham, who had earlier joined in the indignant outcry so copiously publicized in that journal against my 'attack' on Snow (which it had, at its own request, printed), ends a subsequent review of a German author with this:

She was used to well-being, yet it is materialism for the mass of people to get used to well-being. This is a familiar resentment and envy, often seen in Britain, that working people should be going to Florence and Majorca, and buying Beethoven long-playing records. This ought not to be dressed up as moral indignation.[1]

Of course it oughtn't, as far as it exists. And possibly the writer could back her 'familiar' by adducing instances known to her. But to suggest that such resentment and envy are representative, so that she can reasonably dismiss in this way all questioning uneasiness about the human consequences of the technological revolution and the affluent society – is that to promote clear vision and intelligent thought? The unrealism, the disturbing emotional intention, or perversity, betrays itself clearly enough in those 'Beethoven long-playing records'. I myself, after an un-affluent and very much 'engaged' academic life, am not familiar with Majorca or Florence, but in those once very quiet places very much nearer Cambridge to which my wife and I used to take our children the working-class people now everywhere to be met with in profusion carry transistors round with them almost invariably. The music that comes from these, like that one hears in greater volume in the neighbourhood of the bingo establishments (of which the smallest coast-hamlet has at least one – bingo being the most pathetic of vacuum-fillers) doesn't at all suggest aspirations towards Beethoven. If working-class people did, characteristically, or in significant numbers, show a bent that way, who would be found deploring it? – except, of course, Kingsley Amis and his admirers (and there you *have* a significant cultural phenomenon that Miss Gainham would do well to ponder). But as for the actual working-class people who *can* be regarded as characteristic, it's not anything in the nature of moral indignation one feels towards *them*, but shame, concern and apprehension at the way our civilization has let them down – left them to enjoy a 'high standard of living' in a vacuum of disinheritance. The concern, I imagine, is what all decent people capable of sympathetic perception must feel; the apprehension is for the future of humanity.

I shall hardly be accused of paradox here. It isn't very long since the *New Statesman* – *the New Statesman*, on whose Board of Directors it was natural for Snow to be, came out with a front-page article headed 'The Menace of Leisure'. That is an irony indeed – a richly charged one. I recall a passage of D. H. Lawrence's criticism which is especially useful to those faced with enforcing the point that Lawrence was no more given to Morrisian archaizing – garden-suburb handicraftiness – than to the Carlylean gospel of Work. The passage occurs in the 'Study of Thomas Hardy' which deserves more attention than it gets, and is to be found on page 425 of *Phoenix*:

But why so much: why repeat so often the mechanical movement? Let me not have so much of this work to do, let me not be consumed so overmuch in my own self-preservation, let me not be imprisoned in this proven, finite existence all my days.

This has been the cry of humanity since the world began. This is the glamour of kings, the glamour of men who had the opportunity to be . . .

Wherefore I do honour to the machine and to its inventors.[2]

An irony! Lawrence in 1915 does honour to the machine because it gives us leisure – leisure for living (and 'living', he adds, 'is not simply not dying'), and now, for the *New Statesman*, leisure is a menace.

But my immediate point regards the way in which any writer who is known as taking a less simple view of the development and human significance of industrial civilization than Lord Snow (or Lord Robbins) is dubbed

'Luddite', after the machine-breakers, and dismissed – the implication, or contention, being that literature tends in general to be the enemy of enlightenment in this matter. The term has come significantly into favour these last two or three years. Thus Lawrence is a Luddite. And not so long ago I read in the *Sunday Times* (or the other one of those British Sunday papers which have magazine sections in which culture gets a show) a book-notice in which the reviewer, discussing a work on the Victorian city, reeled off a list of names of distinguished Victorian writers as those of notorious Luddites in their attitude towards the new kind of urban development.[3]

Well, though I think it serves no intelligent purpose to dub Carlyle and Ruskin 'Luddites', I could pass that with a shrug. And if Morris is dubbed 'Luddite', it doesn't move me to fierce indignation. But Arnold and Dickens! I will confine my necessarily brief commentary to Dickens, the great creative writer, for it is the dismissal of him that is most significant – I mean most revealing of the nature of the *parti pris* we have to do with in the general dismissal by the Neo-Wellsians of the thought and witness and the profoundly relevant creative energy represented by literature.

Dickens was a great novelist, and, as such, an incomparable social historian. It is the great novelists above all who give us our social history; compared with what is done in *their* work – their creative work – the histories of the professional social historian seem empty and unenlightening. Dickens himself lived intensely, experienced intensely at first hand a wide range of the life of his time, and was peculiarly well qualified to make the most of his opportunities of observing. His power of evoking contemporary reality so that it lives for us today wasn't a mere matter of vividness in rendering the surface; it went with the insight and intelligence of genius. The vitality of his art was understanding. In fact, as I have gone on reading him I have come to realize that his genius is in certain essential ways akin to Lawrence's.[4] He saw how the diverse interplaying currents of life flowed strongly and gathered force here, dwindled there from importance to relative unimportance, settled there into something oppressively stagnant, reasserted themselves elsewhere as strong new promise. The forty years of his writing life were years of portentous change, and, in the way only a great creative writer, sensitive to the full actuality of contemporary life, could, he registers changing England in the succession of his books with wonderful vividness.

Except in so far as Coketown in *Hard Times* constitutes an exception, Dickens doesn't deal with the industrial city. The urban world of modern civilization for him is London. And it is true that he presents it as a squalid, gloomy and oppressive immensity, blighting and sinister to the life it swarms with. But to make this justify our classing Dickens as a Luddite is an odd – significantly odd – proceeding. How much less than no excuse there is for it can be brought out by recalling that in *Dombey and Son*, Dickens's first great novel – one the organizing theme of which entails a critical presentment of the contemporary civilization, the time being that of the triumphant arrival of the railway age, he symbolizes the human purpose and energy that must be looked to for an escape from the squalor, misery and confusion by the railway.[5] There is that expedition in Chapter VI – Polly Toodle, Paul's nurse, with Paul and Florence and Susan Nipper – to

Staggs's Gardens. On their way there they pass through the scene of the great earthquake that has rent Camden Town, where the new railway is being driven through to Euston terminus. The evocation of the scene is a magnificent and characteristic triumph of the Dickensian genius. As I have noted in writing about the book, we are reminded of those drawings, paintings and engravings in which the artists of that time record their sense of the Titanism and romantic sublimity of the works of man. It is not merely by the Titanic audacity, but by the human promise above all, that Dickens is so profoundly impressed. He concludes:

In short, the yet unfinished and unopened Railroad was in Progress, and from the very core of all this dire disorder trailed smoothly away upon its mighty course of civilization and improvement.

Dickens, the Luddite! – the note of this climactic sentence is not a casual inspiration, alien to the force and feeling of *Dombey and Son*. We have a dramatic presence, unmistakably essential to the book, and central here, in Toodle's answer to Dombey's questioning when Polly Toodle, his wife (the natural motherly woman, and as such herself essential to Dickens's creative theme), is being interviewed as the prospective wet-nurse who shall save little Paul's life: what has Toodle's work been? –

'Mostly underground, Sir, till I got married. I came to the level then. I'm agoing on one of these here railroads, when they comes into full play.'

The prosperity and happiness of the Toodle family are associated with the coming into full play of the railways, and seen as a representative accompaniment.

By way of insisting that this characteristic of *Dombey and Son* is characteristic of Dickens, I will just point to Daniel Doyce, the inventor, and his place in the scheme of values of *Little Dorrit*, that very great novel which, of all Dickens's larger works, is the most highly organized, everything in it being significant in relation to the whole – and the whole constituting something like an inquest into civilization in contemporary England.[6] Doyce, genius of beneficent invention, and, in the face of the Circumlocution Office and the patronizing bourgeois (Meagles), invincibly sane, persistent and matter-of-fact, pairs with Cavalletto, the little Italian who puzzles the inhabitants of Bleeding Heart Yard by his simple ability to live and enjoy the sun: neither a major actor, they are major presences for the dramatic and poetic process of valuation implicit in Dickens's art because of what they so potently are and represent.

What I have been trying to bring out for clear recognition is the element of deep-seated refusal to perceive that betrays itself in such characteristic instances as I have adduced. We have it not only in the dead set at eliminating literature and what it represents from all serious relevance to the issues, but in the attitude towards *any* suggestion that the issues are essentially more complex than Snow's Rede lecture would make them, and fraught with other kinds of menace to humanity than he is able to recognize. There is that business of 'the old wheelwright's shop' – the play made with that phrase, thrown out with a knowing 'ha-ha' in the voice and manner, by a well-known Cambridge figure of the BBC world.[7] The ironist is what Snow calls a 'literary intellectual', and the blind set of the will he relies on and means to confirm is that which had a representative illustration when a bright lady journalist in the *Spectator* quite wantonly dragged my name in as that (everyone knew) of the man to apply to if you wanted a wistful lament for the Old Style Pub (now vanished, I gather – for actually I know nothing about these things).[8] The sole factual basis that could be alleged for these insinuations is the use to which, thirty years ago and more, Denys Thompson and myself in *Culture and Environment*, a book for schools, put George Sturt's *The Wheelwright's Shop*.[9]

The use to which we put Sturt had nothing William-Morrisian in it; neither of us, I may say, went in for folk-dancing – or pubs. The attention we aimed at promoting was to the present, and our emphasis was on the need to understand the nature of the accelerating and inevitable change that was transforming our civilization. The wheelwright's business, we pointed out, or noted how Sturt pointed out, didn't merely provide him with a satisfying craft that entailed the use of a diversity of skills; it contained a full human meaning in itself – it kept a human significance always present, and this was a climate in which the craftsman lived and worked: lived *as* he worked. Its materials were for the most part locally grown, and the wheelwright quite commonly had noted as a tree *in situ* the timber that came to the shop – which is a representative aspect of the general truth. The customers too were local, and he knew them, themselves and their settings, as meeting their particular requirements he had to, individually – he, the wheelwright of the neighbourhood. He saw the products of his craft in use, serving their functions in the life and purpose of a community that really *was* a community, a human microcosm, and couldn't help feeling itself one.

We didn't recall this organic kind of relation of work to life in any nostalgic spirit, as something to be restored, or to take a melancholy pleasure in lamenting; but by way of emphasizing that it was *gone*, with the organic community it belonged to, not to be restored in any foreseeable future. We were calling attention to an essential change in human conditions that is entailed by the accelerating technological revolution, and to the nature of the attendant human problem. And our sense that the problem was not likely to get all the attention it should be seen as demanding has been redundantly justified.

It is plain that the kind of relation between work and living documented in *The Wheelwright's Shop*, or anything like it, can't by any serious mind be proposed as an ideal aim in *our* world; that the only bearing it has on the possibilities we have to consider is that to recognize the nature of the change is to recognize the nature of the challenge, the problem that Snow ignores, a frightening characteristic that it has being to escape notice for what it is.

Mr Toodle of *Dombey and Son*, as stoker and aspiring engine-driver, had a job out of which he got much satisfaction, besides that of being able to support his family. He had there, we know, an advantage over the mass of industrial workers, and we have no difficulty in understanding how Dickens could present him as invested with a cheering significance for the human future. But the future we now see for the Toodleses is automation, and the future seen as automation is what makes the *New Statesman* talk of the 'menace of leisure'. The development by which, for industrial workers, real living tends to be something thought of as saved for the leisure part of life is soon to be consummated. The meaninglessness, or human emptiness, of work will be sufferable because the working part of life will be comparatively short and the leisure part preponderant.

That this upshot of technological progress needs to be thought of as facing us with a problem is, as I've noted, receiving some kind of recognition: 'the menace of leisure', 'education for leisure', and so on – phrases of that kind give us the nature of the recognition. And my point is that such recognition is no real recognition of the problem that faces humanity. Certainly that problem is not being recognized for what it really is when discussion proceeds in terms of the need to educate for positive and more satisfying uses of his leisure the worker whose routine work, requiring or permitting no creative effort on his part, and no large active interest – little more, in fact, than automatisms – leaves him incapable of any but the passive and the crude.

We are *all* involved – and in the most intimate, inward and essential way; and not merely by reason of congested roads, the smell of fish and chips, the ubiquity of transistors and that kind of inconvenience, which is what, in England, discussion pertaining to the ethos of the *New Statesman* tends, however democratically (of course), to suggest. A general impoverishment of life – that is the threat that, ironically, accompanies the technological advance and the rising standard of living; and we are all involved.

Snow gives us a pregnant demonstration, very pertinent to the explaining of what I mean, when, as himself representative of his Two Cultures, he posits, to be set over against what he calls the 'scientific culture', a 'literary culture' that he represents by the literary intellectual of the *New Statesman* milieu, or the modish London literary world. Well, our traditional culture hasn't yet been finally reduced, though Snow in his Rede lecture reduces it, to *that*. But his being able to do it quite naturally, without a thought of being questioned, shows where we have got. And the process so exemplified – I permit myself to say what should be obvious – affects the scientist, the scientist as a man, as nearly and intimately as anyone.

I say it, because no one will suggest that *he*, the real scientist (or the technological expert, for that matter), is to be thought of as sharing the state of the human quasi-automaton – the human or animal or organic adjunct to automation. The scientist very well may – the creative kind certainly will – derive great satisfaction from his work. But he cannot derive from it all that a human being needs – intellectually, spiritually, culturally. Yet to think of a distinguished mind having to go for refreshment, edification and nourishment to the 'literary culture' represented by Snow's 'literary intellectual' and identified by Snow with 'the traditional culture' is painful and depressing – unbearably humiliating to some of us. For I was speaking responsibly when I said in my Richmond lecture that Snow's 'literary intellectual' is an enemy of art and life. He belongs to the cultural conditions that make it seem plausible – obvious good sense – to talk about 'The Two Cultures'.

The term 'culture', of course, like most important words, has more forces than one in which it can be used for intellectually respectable purposes; but even if Snow had not with naïve explicitness identified one of his pair with 'the traditional culture', the fair and final dismissing comment on his Rede lecture as offering serious thought about the problem he points to (but doesn't see) would be: 'there is only *one* culture; to talk of *two* in your way is to use an essential term with obviously disqualifying irresponsibility'. It is obviously absurd to posit a 'culture' that the scientist has *qua* scientist. What Snow proposes to condemn the scientist to when he points to the really educated man as combining the 'two cultures', what he condemns the scientist to for his cultural needs – his non-scientific *human* needs, is (in the British terms I am familiar with) the culture of the *New Statesman* and the Sunday papers, which is what Snow's 'literary intellectual' actually represents. And for that I have intimated my contempt. No serious problem or theme is being tackled when an alleged 'scientific culture' is being placed against *that* as the complementary reality.

The difficulty about proceeding now on a more positive line is that the issues, being basic, are so large, complex and difficult to limit, and that (a distinctive mark of the present phase of civilization) even in talking to a highly educated audience there is so little one can take as given and granted and understood to be necessarily granted. One can only be clear about one's focal interest and determine one's course and one's economy in relation to that. Mine – ours, may I say? – is the university; that is, the function and the idea.

It may be commented at this point that I am not absolved from explaining what positively I mean by 'culture' in the sense I invoke when I criticize misleading uses of the term. I won't proceed by attempting to offer a direct formal definition; that wouldn't conduce to economy, or to the kind of clarity that for the present purpose we need. Faced with the problem of indicating clearly the nature of my answer to questions about meaning, I recall Snow's account of the supremely creative human achievement present to us in Science, and the comment it moved me to. This is Snow: 'As though the scientific edifice of the physical world', he exclaims, 'were not, in its intellectual depth, complexity and articulation, the most beautiful and wonderful collective work of the mind of man.' My comment was: 'It is pleasant to think of Snow contemplating, daily perhaps, the intellectual depth, complexity and articulation in all their beauty. But there is a prior human achievement of collaborative creation, a more basic work of the mind of man (and more than the mind), one without which the triumphant erection of the scientific edifice would not have been possible: that is, the creation of the human world, including language.'

This is surely a clear enough truth, and I don't suppose anyone here wants to dispute it. The trouble is that in our time, when we need as no other age did before to see that it is given full conscious realizing recognition, there seems to be something like an impossibility of getting anything better than a mere notional assent. Can we without exaggeration say, for instance, that it was even that in the *Guardian* first leader which I read when, a couple of years ago, my thoughts were very much on the theme I am discussing now? The leader, though characteristic enough, a little surprised me, for I had had strong grounds for supposing the *Guardian* pro-Snow and anti-Leavis – committed to the view that there was nothing to be said for my side in the notorious so-called 'debate'. But this leader, dealing with Mr Harold Wilson's 'vision of the future' at Scarborough, remarked that 'even a C. P. Snow would be a poor substitute for an informed and open discussion of the uses to be made of science', and that it 'would ... be a tragedy if either party gave as its chief reason for a further extension of the universities the need to recruit more scientists'. It concluded: 'Science is a means to an end.'[10]

'Science is a means to an end': what more could one ask? – it concedes everything. You'll reply that 'concedes' is an infelicitous word, the proposition being a truism. Yes, a truism: there's the rub. But 'rub' itself is an infelicitous word: it doesn't – quite the contrary – suggest what I am calling attention to, which is the absence, where 'ends' are adverted to as needing some consideration, of the friction, the sense of pregnant arrest, which goes with active realizing thought and the taking of a real charged meaning. 'Science is a means to an end': yes – a rising standard of living. I perpetrate my notorious exhibition of bad manners at poor Lord Snow's expense, or, as I myself should put it, do my best to get some recognition for the inadequacy of that accepted formula as representing a due concern for human ends (a matter, it seems to me, of great urgency), and I get for response a vast deal of blackguarding, misrepresentation and contemptuous dismissal, and then the *Spectator* offering to strike a *juste milieu* between my Richmond lecture on the one hand and Aldous Huxley offering to strike a *juste milieu* between me and Snow on the other.[11] The *Spectator*, pointing out how unsatisfactory Huxley is, endorses by making it its own his attribution to me of 'one-track, moralistic literarism'. To set over against Snow's deviation, scientism, you see, there is mine, which is literarism.

I'll leave aside for a moment this curious term, which Huxley, with an American distribution of stress and quantity (after all he, though the *Spectator* challenges for itself with the term the genuine and solid middle position it was meant to claim for him, invented it) found perhaps more speakable than I do. Immediately in place is to insist on the truth – not, unhappily, a truism – that once the naïvety that takes 'rising standard of living' to represent an adequate concern for human ends has been transcended, the determination of what, adequately conceived, they *are* is seen to be very far from simple. Human nature and need are certainly more complex than Lord Snow assumes. They won't be fully apparent for recognition in any present of any society. The most carefully analysed and interpreted answers to the most cunningly framed questionnaires, the most searching and thorough sociological surveys, won't yield an adequate account of what they are.

And 'end' itself, though a word that we most certainly have to use in the kind of context and the kind of way I've been exemplifying, tends, perhaps, to turn the receptivity of the mind away from orders of consideration that are essential – essential, that is, when the criteria for determining how we should discriminate and judge in the face of a rapidly changing civilization are what we want to bring to full consciousness. Mankind, for instance, has a need to feel life significant; a hunger for significance that isn't altogether satisfied by devotion to Tottenham Hotspur or by hopes of the World Cup for a team called England or Uruguay, or by space travel (mediated by professional publicists), or by patriotic ardour nourished on international athletics, or by the thrill of broken records – even though records, by dint of scientific training, go on being broken and the measurement of times becomes progressively finer.

If, of course, one is challenged to stand and deliver and say what 'significance' is – 'If you use the term you ought to be able to say what you mean by it!' – it is hardly possible to answer convincingly at the level of the challenge. But that is far from saying that the matter for consideration raised with the term is not, when thought turns on human ends, of the greatest moment. And that 'high standard of living' expresses a dangerously inadequate notion or criterion of human prosperity is a simple enough truth.

Now, if we are asked how we are to arrive – for ourselves, in the first place, but of course, not merely that – at a more adequate notion, the answer, it seems to me, clearly is: when human ends require to be pondered in relation to the pressing problems and opportunities with which our civilization faces us, one's thinking should not be blind to the insights given in cultural tradition – on the contrary, it should be informed with the knowledge of basic human need that is transmitted by *that*. This is not a simple answer; no serious answer *could* be. I have used the phrase 'cultural tradition' rather than Snow's 'the traditional culture', because this last suggests something quite different from what I mean. It suggests something belonging to the past, a reservoir of alleged wisdom, an established habit, an unadventurousness in the face of life and change. Let me, as against that, extend briefly the quotation I've permitted myself from my Richmond lecture. Having, in comment on Snow's claim regarding the 'scientific edifice of the physical world', pointed to the 'prior human achievement of collaborative creation ... the creation of the human world, including language', I go on: 'It is one we cannot rest on as on something done in the past. It lives in the living creative response to change in the present.' A little further on, insisting on the antithesis to what 'traditional' usually suggests, I put it in this way, and the formulation gives me what I need now: 'for the sake of our humanity – our humanness, for the sake of a human future we must do, with intelligent resolution and with faith, all we can to maintain the full life in the present – and life is growth – of our transmitted culture'.

We have no other; there is only one, and there can be no substitute. Those who talk of two and of joining them would present us impressively with the sum of two nothings: it is the void the modern world tackles with drugs, sex and alcohol.* That kind of sage doesn't touch on the real problem; he has no cognizance of it. It is a desperately difficult problem; I don't pretend to know of comfortable answers and easy solutions. Simply I believe that in respect of this problem, too, intelligence-directed human effort has *its* part to play, and that there is a human instinct of self-preservation to be appealed to.

In my Richmond lecture, recalling a formulation I had been prompted to in the old days, when the Marxising expositors of human affairs thronged the arena, I remarked that there is a certain autonomy of the human spirit. I didn't mean by that to suggest that the higher non-material achievements of human culture, the achievements of collaborative creation that belong most obviously to what I call in discussion the 'third realm', were

_____
* And, I can now add, 'student unrest' and the vote and majority-status at eighteen.

to be thought of as spontaneous, unconditioned expressions of an intrinsic human nature sprouting or creating gratuitously, in a realm of pure spirit. I was merely insisting that there *is* an intrinsic human nature, with needs and latent potentialities the most brilliant scientist may very well be blank about, and the technologically directed planner may ignore – with (it doesn't need arguing) disastrous consequences. Of course, the collaborative creation of the world of significances and values has to be seen as a matter of response to material conditions and economic necessities.

Let me repeat, however, that I didn't thirty years ago point to the state of affairs, the relation between cultural values (or – shall I say? – human significances) and economic fact, documented in *The Wheelwright's Shop* – which I've hardly mentioned these thirty years – as something we should aim at recovering; but as something finally gone. That relation was an essential condition of the kind of achievement of the higher culture (spiritual, intellectual, humane) that is represented by Shakespeare's works. Such a relation, for any world we can foresee, is gone.

Technological change has marked cultural consequences. There is an implicit logic that will impose, if not met by creative intelligence and corrective purpose, simplifying and reductive criteria of human need and human good, and generate, to form the mind and spirit of civilization, disastrously false and inadequate conceptions of the *ends* to which science should be a means. This logic or drive is immensely and insidiously powerful. Its tendency appears very plainly in the cultural effects of mass-production – in the levelling-down that goes with standardization. Ponder, I find myself saying in England, to academic audiences, the 'magazine sections' of the Sunday papers (they know which two I mean), and tell yourselves that *this*, for many dons – and I am thinking of the non-scientists, the custodians of culture – represents the top level: what Arnold meant by 'the best that is thought and known in our time'. It will almost certainly represent the top level for those who, at this time of rapid and confident and large-scale reforms, make the authoritative and decisive recommendations in the field of higher education.

To point out these things is not to be a Luddite. It is to insist on the truth that, in an age of revolutionary and constantly advancing technology, the sustained collaborative devotion of directed energy and directing intelligence that is science needs to be accompanied by another, and quite different, devotion of purpose and energy, another sustained collaborative effort of creative intelligence. I will again quote what I actually said in the offending lecture: 'the advance of science and technology means a human future of change so rapid and of such kinds, of tests and challenges so unprecedented, of decisions and possible non-decisions so momentous and insidious in their consequences, that mankind – this is surely clear – will need to be in full intelligent possession of its full humanity ... What we need, and shall continue to need not less, is something with the livingness of the deepest vital instinct; as intelligence, a power – rooted, strong in experience, and supremely human – of creative response to the new challenges of time; something that is alien to both of Snow's cultures.'

What I have been pointing out is that we shall not have this power if provision is not made for a more conscious and deliberate fostering of it than has characterized our civilization in the past. And here comes in my concern for the idea of the university as a focus of consciousness and human responsibility.

I must close on the note of transition, for I can't here follow up this opening. My mention of the idea of the university is a concluding emphasis on the positive; an insistence that my attitude is very much a positive one, and that I *have* a positive theme for the development of which I am fully charged – a theme intent on practice. Of course, I speak – have been speaking (that was plain – and was expected of me) – as an Englishman, and my 'engaged' preoccupation with the idea of the university has a British context, the tight little island of Mr Harold Wilson's premiership and Lord Robbins's Report on Higher Education.[12] Yet I can't think of the differences between the situation I face at home in England and the situation in America (which, as I've remarked, is not a tight little island) without telling myself with conviction that we face in essence one and the same problem, and that the widest community of the intelligently concerned that can be made aware of itself and of the menace will not be too large. I have reason for knowing, with encouragement and gratitude, that there are many Americans who feel the same.

The special bent of my positive concern is given when I gloss 'the university as a focus of consciousness and human responsibility' by 'the university as a guarantor of a real performance of the critical function – that critical function which is a creative one'. It is here, of course, that I am supposed to have laid myself open to the charge of 'literarism' – for it is obviously meant to be a charge. Its suggestion is very much that of the writer in the *Melbourne Quarterly* who, in a quite flattering article, said I sometimes seem to think that literary criticism will save us.[13] The possibility of this irony meaning anything seems to depend on a conception of literary criticism that, when I try, I can't conceive – it eludes me.

For – and this is my reply to Aldous Huxley as well – I don't believe in any 'literary values', and you won't find me talking about them; the judgments the literary critic is concerned with are judgments about life. What the critical discipline is concerned with is relevance and precision in making and developing them. To think that to have a vital contemporary performance of the critical function matters is to think that creative literature matters; and it matters because to have a living literature, a literary tradition that *lives* in the present – and nothing lives unless it goes on being creative, is to have, as an informing spirit in civilization, an informed, charged and authoritative awareness of inner human nature and human need.

In my discussions of the university English School as a liaison centre I have been intent on enforcing my conviction as to the kind of effort by which we must promote the growth of that power of which I have just spoken: 'a power – rooted, strong in experience and supremely human – of creative response to the new challenges of time; something that is alien to both of Snow's cultures'. My concern for the idea of an English School isn't to be thought of as just a matter of syllabus, teaching methods and a given kind of student product to be turned out. The educational problem itself in that narrow sense conduces to discouragement, despair and cynicism when approached merely in those terms.

But I won't now develop that observation beyond saying that one's essential concern should conceive itself as being to make the university what it ought to be – something (that is) more than a collocation of specialist departments: a centre of consciousness for the community. The problem is to re-establish an effective educated public, for it is only in the existence of an educated public, capable of responding and making its response felt, that 'standards' can be there for the critic to appeal to. This is true not merely of literary criticism; the literary-critical judgment is the type of all judgments and valuations belonging to what in my unphilosophical way I've formed the habit of calling the 'third realm' – the collaboratively created human world, the realm of what is *neither* public in the sense belonging to science (it can't be weighed or tripped over or brought into the laboratory or pointed to) *nor* merely private and personal (consider the nature of a language, of the language we can't do without – and literature is a manifestation of language). One's aim is that the university itself, having a real and vital centre of consciousness, should *be* such a public or community as the critic needs, being in that way one of the sustaining creative nuclei of a larger community.

One might then hope that one might, at Cambridge, for example – my own university (and Lord Snow's and Lord Annan's) – get the effective response when one uttered the appropriate judgment on the publicizers, public relations men, heads of houses, academic ward-bosses, hobnobbers with Cabinet ministers, who are planning, they tell us, to remodel the University and start going a new kind of higher education. Might...might, if...if...; but don't take me to be suggesting that the actuality and the blind enlightened menace are anything but what they are. Let me end with a sentence and a bit from Lord Robbins of the Robbins Report:

> Since Sir Charles Snow's Rede lecture, we have heard a great deal of the two cultures in this country; for reasons which I completely fail to understand, Sir Charles's very moderate indication of danger arouses very high passions. To me his diagnosis seems obvious ... [14]

To me it seems obvious that Snow's *raison d'être* is to be an elementary test.

NOTES

The following notes identify references or explain allusions where they may not be clear from the text itself. They do not seek to gloss every proper name or citation, and they do not provide page references to the many quotations from Snow's Rede lecture.

'Two Cultures?'

1. These were two of Snow's tests for scientific literacy; see C. P. Snow, *The Two Cultures*, ed. Stefan Collini (Cambridge University Press, 1993), pp. 30, 15.
2. In Britain's highly selective secondary education system at this time, a small number of sixth-formers in the intellectually most ambitious schools were given special preparation for scholarship examinations for Oxford and Cambridge; Leavis marked the scripts of those applying to read English at Downing College.
3. See William Cooper (pseud. of H. S. Hoff), *C. P. Snow* (London: Published for the British Council and the National Book League by Longmans, Green, 1959).
4. The most celebrated of Snow's novels was a fictionalized account of the election of the head of his own college (Christ's): *The Masters* (1951).
5. The plot of *The Affair* (1960) turns on a miscarriage of justice in which a young science fellow is charged with scientific fraud and dismissed from his college.
6. Lewis Eliot was the central character in the 'Strangers and Brothers' sequence of eleven novels which Snow published between 1940 and 1970; *Corridors of Power* (1963) was the

ninth of the sequence, and helped to give general currency to the title phrase.

7. Rupert Birkin is the character who most represents the author's views in *Women in Love* (1920). Leavis had consistently championed D. H. Lawrence's genius from 1930 onwards, and he gave his fullest assessment of Lawrence's 'supreme' novel in *D. H. Lawrence, Novelist* (London: Chatto, 1955).

8. Joseph Conrad's *The Shadow Line: A Confession* (1917) focusses on the experience of a young officer taking command of his first ship. Leavis's fullest analysis, and praise, of Conrad's works had been given in *The Great Tradition: George Eliot, Henry James, Joseph Conrad* (London: Chatto, 1948).

9. Tom Brangwen is one of the central characters in Lawrence's novel, *The Rainbow* (1915). *The Rainbow* and *Women in Love* had initially been conceived as a single story before being recast as two separate books.

10. For the distinction between 'wealth' and 'well-being', see John Ruskin, *Unto This Last* (1862), esp. essay IV.

11. In a speech in 1957, Harold Macmillan, the British prime minister, said that 'most of our people have never had it so good', which was popularly reported in the form 'you've never had it so good'. See Peter Hennessy, *Having It So Good: Britain in the 1950s* (London: Allen Lane, 2006), 'Overture'.

12. Anonymous review of Georges Friedmann, *The Anatomy of Work*, in *Economist* (2 December 1961), 898–9.

13. Leavis had elaborated his understanding of the character of literary criticism, including the central form of 'This is so, isn't it?', in numerous publications; one frequently cited instance was in 'Literary criticism and philosophy: a reply', *Scrutiny* 6 (1937), 59–70; reprinted in *The Common Pursuit* (London: Chatto, 1952).

14. Leavis developed his notion of 'the third realm' in his article 'Valuation in criticism' (1966), reprinted in *Valuation in Criticism and Other Essays* (Cambridge University Press, 1986), and most fully in *The Living Principle: 'English' as a Discipline of Thought* (London: Chatto, 1975).

15. Leavis had most fully expounded his ideas on the place of English in university studies in his *Education and the University: A Sketch for an 'English School'* (London: Chatto, 1943).

16. Leavis and a small group of associates edited the journal *Scrutiny* from 1932 to 1953.

17. F. R. Leavis, *New Bearings in English Poetry* (London: Chatto, 1932), and *D. H. Lawrence* (Cambridge: Minority Press, 1930).

18. Lionel Trilling, 'Science, literature, and culture: a comment on the Leavis–Snow controversy', *Commentary* (June 1962), 461–77.

19. Richard Wollheim, 'London letter', *Partisan Review* 29 (1962), 267–9.

20. In the first batch of correspondence printed by the *Spectator* after Leavis's lecture, Dame Edith Sitwell wrote: 'Is it possible that Sir Charles may have offended Dr Leavis by the fact of his great fame, or by the fact that he – Sir Charles – can write English? Only this can explain such a silly exhibition.' *Spectator* (16 March 1962), 331.

21. Subsequent research has confirmed that this was far from being a ridiculous conjecture; see Guy Ortolano, *The Two Cultures Controversy: Science, Literature, and Cultural Politics in Postwar Britain* (Cambridge University Press, 2009), esp. pp. 117–26.

'Luddites?'

1. Sarah Gainham, 'Correspondence', *Spectator* (23 March 1962), 356; Sarah Gainham, review of Gudrun Tempel,

Speaking Frankly About the Germans, in *Spectator* (30 August 1963), 265.

2. D. H. Lawrence, 'Study of Thomas Hardy' (1915), in *Phoenix: The Posthumous Papers of D. H. Lawrence*, ed. Edward D. McDonald (London: Heinemann, 1936), p. 425.

3. The author welcomed the book under review as providing an alternative view of the period to 'those who prefer to exercise their social nostalgia and rural homesickness in fond remembrance of a golden, if bogus, past, On this score history provides a welcome antidote to literature. Those natural Luddites – Dickens, Ruskin, Morris and Carlyle – had a field day'. The review concluded that the presentation of the case for progress in the book 'makes a welcome change from the recent ignorant splutterings of some of the Leavisite school.' Neil McKendrick, 'Chamberlain's Birmingham' (review of Asa Briggs, *Victorian Cities*), *Sunday Times* (8 November 1963), 30. McKendrick, a younger Cambridge historian, was a protegé and intimate friend of Snow's close ally, J. H. Plumb.

4. Notoriously, Leavis had for some years held a somewhat disparaging view of Dickens, maintaining (in *The Great Tradition*) that his 'genius was that of a great entertainer', but he progressively came to regard him as one of the major English novelists. This later view is stated most fully in the book coauthored with Q. D. Leavis, *Dickens the Novelist* (London: Chatto, 1970).

5. Leavis first developed this very positive assessment of *Dombey and Son* in 'Dombey and Son', *Sewanee Review* 70 (1962), 177–201.

6. In the revised edition of *The Great Tradition*, published in 1960, Leavis added a note (p. 19) saying: 'I now think that, if any one writer can be said to have created the modern novel, it is Dickens, and that *Little Dorrit* is one of the great European novels.'

7. Endorsing Snow's attack on the nostalgia of literary intellectuals in general, Graham Hough, a colleague of Leavis's
in the Cambridge English faculty and frequent reviewer
and broadcaster, observed: 'We shall all soon be as dead
as the old wheelwright's shop'. Graham Hough, 'Crisis
in literary education', *Sunday Times* (17 March 1963.), 26;
reprinted in J. H. Plumb (ed.), *Crisis in the Humanities* (Harmondsworth: Penguin, 1964), p. 96. The reference was to
'George Bourne' (pseudonym for George Sturt), *The Wheelwright's Shop* (1923), cited by Leavis at p. 97.
8. 'One has to admit that the origins of pub atmosphere
are lost in the roseate pre-history charted best by Dr
Leavis'. Maureen O'Connor, 'No longer the local', *Spectator*
(3 May 1963), 585–6. Leavis responded in a letter the following week (601), pointing out that the sneer was unwarranted and not based on anything to be found in his work,
adding: 'To insist on the need to promote a common awareness of the nature of the immense changes being brought
about in our civilisation, and of the danger of an unconscious acquiescence in the human impoverishment that may,
unrecognised as such, attend automatically on a technological progress towards a civilisation of "more jam" is not to
indulge in, or to promote, or in any way to favour, romanc-
ing about the past.'
9. Leavis and Denys Thompson coauthored *Culture and Environment: The Training of Critical Awareness* in 1933, a practical manual designed for use in schools and colleges. Critics
subsequently made much of its invocation of 'the organic
community', as well as of its use of Sturt, though these
themes figured relatively little in Leavis's later writing.
10. 'Over the hills, not far away', *Guardian* (2 October 1963),
10. Harold Wilson, the newly elected leader of the Labour
Party, made a speech at the party's annual conference at
Scarborough, one (misquoted) phrase of which about 'the

white heat of the technological revolution' became famous. Wilson actually said that 'in all our plans for the future, we are redefining and we are restating our Socialism in terms of the scientific revolution... The Britain that is going to be forged in the white heat of this revolution will be no place for restrictive practices or for outdated methods on either side of industry'. Harold Wilson, *Purpose in Politics: Selected Speeches* (London: Weidenfeld & Nicolson, 1964), p. 27.

11. See Aldous Huxley, *Literature and Science* (1963); 'The scientific nightingale', *Spectator* (4 October 1963), 406.

12. *Higher Education: Report of the Committee Appointed by the Prime Minister under the Chairmanship of Lord Robbins, 1961–1963* (London: HMSO, 1963; cmnd 2154).

13. Leavis's reference is, as so often, somewhat inexact, but it seems probable that this refers to Vincent Buckley, 'Leavis and his "line"', *Melbourne Critical Review* (subsequently *Critical Review*) 8 (1965), 110–20, esp. 117.

14. Lionel Robbins, 'The fine and applied arts at university level' (1964), in *The University in the Modern World, and Other Papers on Higher Education* (London: Macmillan, 1966), p. 116 (Leavis slightly misquotes; Robbins wrote: 'To me much of his diagnosis seems obvious').